Applying Research Knowledge

To Accompany the Following Books

- ✔ ANASTAS, J.W. & MacDONALD, M.L. (1994). *Research design for social work and the human services*. New York: Lexington.
- ✔ BABBIE, E.R. (1995). *The practice of social research* (7th ed.). Belmont, CA: Wadsworth.
- ✔ BAILEY, K.D. (1994). *Methods of social research* (4th ed.). New York: Free Press.
- ✔ DePOY, E. & GITLIN, L.N. (1994). *Introduction to research*. St. Louis, MO: Mosby.
- ✔ FRANKFORT-NACHMIAS, C. & NACHMIAS, D. (1992). *Research methods in the social sciences* (4th ed.). New York: St. Martin's Press.
- ✔ GRINNELL, R.M., JR. (Ed.) (1993). *Social work research and evaluation* (4th ed.). Itasca, IL: F.E. Peacock.
- ✔ JUDD, C.M., SMITH E.R., & KIDDER, L.H. (1991). *Research methods in social relations* (6th ed.). Fort Worth, TX: Harcourt Brace Jovanovich.
- ✔ LEEDY, P.D. (1993). *Practical research* (5th ed.). New York: Macmillan.
- ✔ MARLOW, C. (1993). *Research methods for generalist social work*. Pacific Grove, CA: Brooks/Cole.
- ✔ MONETTE, D.R., SULLIVAN, T.J., & DeJONG, C.R. (1994). *Applied social research* (3rd ed.). Fort Worth, TX: Harcourt Brace.
- ✔ NEUMAN, W.L. (1994). *Social research methods* (2nd ed.). Boston, MA: Allyn & Bacon.
- ✔ ROYSE, D.D. (1995). *Research methods in social work* (2nd ed.). Chicago, IL: Nelson-Hall.
- ✔ RUBIN, A. & BABBIE, E. (1993). *Research methods for social work* (2nd ed.). Pacific Grove, CA: Brooks/Cole.
- ✔ SINGLETON, R.A., JR., STRAITS, B.C., & MILLER STRAITS, M. (1993). *Approaches to social research* (2nd ed.). New York: Oxford.
- ✔ WILLIAMS, M., TUTTY, L.M., & GRINNELL, R.M., JR. (1995). *Research in social work* (2nd ed.). Itasca, IL: F.E. Peacock.
- ✔ YEGIDIS, B.L. & WEINBACH, R.W. (1996). *Research methods for social workers* (2nd ed). Boston, MA: Allyn & Bacon.

Applying Research Knowledge

A Workbook for Social Work Students

Second Edition

Robert W. Weinbach
University of South Carolina

Richard M. Grinnell, Jr.
The University of Calgary

Allyn and Bacon
Boston • London • Toronto • Sydney • Tokyo • Singapore

Vice President and Publisher: Susan K. Badger
Executive Editor: Karen Hanson
Managing Editor: Judy Fifer
Editorial Assistant: Jennifer Jacobson
Executive Marketing Manager: Joyce Nilsen
Senior Production Administrator: Marjorie Payne
Manufacturing Buyer: Aloka Rathman
Cover Designer: Jennifer Burns

ISBN: 0-205-19387-0

Printed in the United States of America
10 9 8 7 6 5 4 3 2 1   99 98 97 96 95

Contents

Introduction

THE PAST FEW YEARS have brought a renewed emphasis on effective teaching in colleges and universities. Compared to the past, more emphasis is now being placed on helping students to succeed. One of the many ways to maximize student success is by providing them with relevant and timely feedback. Generally, most instructors utilize a variety of assessment procedures in providing this feedback which range from class presentations, in-class examinations, take-home examinations, essays, quizzes, and critiques.

Students taking research methods courses are usually assessed two or three times in an attempt to discern how well they understand the material. Sometimes these major assessment points are a bit late in helping those students who are struggling in embarrassed silence within the anonymity of large class sections.

To help these students, and instructors alike, we feel weekly indicators, or assessments, of how well the students are doing would be of some help. This *Workbook* is designed to address this need. More specifically, its primary function is to monitor individual student learning while at the same time complementing the course's major exams, papers, etc. If used regularly and conscientiously, this *Workbook* should assist the instructor in the early identification of those students who are "struggling" and need additional help.

RESEARCH METHODS TEXTS

THERE ARE ABOUT 16 books that most social work instructors adopt for their research methods courses. Generally speaking, the books contain essentially the same content. Obviously, each one arranges and emphasizes its content differently than the next—the purpose of its existence. However, they all have two objectives in common. First, they contain core material that is needed for students to appreciate and understand the role of research. Second, they prepare students to conduct basic research studies and to become beginning critical consumers of the professional research literature. Since a majority of the core content of research methods books is so similar, this *Workbook* can be used with any of them.

FEATURES AND USE

✔ It is relatively inexpensive. With the price of tuition and textbooks constantly rising, students cannot be expected to invest a big chunk of their educational budget into a supplemental learning aide such as this one.

✔ It is formatted to compliment the most utilized research methods texts.

✔ The topics, or Units, parallel as much as possible, the sequence of the topics covered within the research methods texts. Topics are clearly identified (see unit overviews) to assist the instructor in assigning the appropriate unit of work.

✔ Unit exercises are printed on perforated paper. This allows them to be used out-of sequence to correspond with the text used.

✔ The first ten questions in each Unit assess a student's understanding of key concepts. The second five questions assess the student's ability to apply these concepts to actual published research studies. While the 15 questions do not test everything that a student should know about a particular topic area, they can suggest whether or not a student has mastered most of the basics and seems to be "on track."

✔ The completed and graded Units can be a valuable aide in reviewing for subsequent major examinations. Thus, we suggest that students be allowed to keep them, at least until the research course is completed.

✔ Each Unit should take only a few minutes for an instructor to review.

✔ A grade (or satisfactory/unsatisfactory) can be awarded for each Unit that could go toward the student's overall course grade. Or, there can be no grade awarded whatsoever.

✔ A Unit can be completed by an individual student or a small group of students.

With the above features in mind, there are two complementary ways in which this *Workbook* can be used.

✔ A Unit can be completed by students at the end of a class session. After specific required readings in the text have been read and the topic has been discussed in class, the first ten questions of the appropriate Unit can be answered by the students. This procedure would provide a quick assessment of the students' comprehension of the text material and corresponding lecture. Or, all of the Unit's 15 questions could be answered and turned in a couple of days after the class.

✔ A Unit can be completed at home (after reading the material in the text) and handed in at the beginning of the next class session or by some assigned date prior to it. This procedure would provide a quick assessment of the students' comprehension of the text material only—before the lecture. After glancing at the students' answers, the instructor would be able to obtain a quick assessment of how well the students knew the material in the text before the lecture begins. If the answers to a "batch" of Units suggest widespread student confusion about an answer to a given question, the instructor could highlight the material that he or she thought was necessary and skim material that the students fully understood.

All in all, the flexibility of this *Workbook* is limited only to the imagination of the research instructor and/or student. Your creative use of this *Workbook* is heavily encouraged.

NEW TO THIS EDITION

✔ We have ***deleted*** one text that appeared in the last edition:

- Adams, G.R. & Schvaneveldt, J.D. (1991). *Understanding research methods* (2nd ed.). White Plains, NY: Longman.

✔ We have ***added*** four texts that did not appear in the last edition:

- Anastas, J.W. & MacDonald, M.L. (1994). *Research design for social work and the human services.* New York: Lexington.

- DePoy, E. & Gitlin, L.N. (1994). *Introduction to research.* St. Louis, MO: Mosby.

- Singleton, R.A., Jr., Straits, B.C., & Miller Straits, M. (1993). *Approaches to social research* (2nd ed.). New York: Oxford.

- Williams, M., Tutty, L.M., & Grinnell, R.M., Jr. (1995). *Research in social work* (2nd ed.). Itasca, IL: F.E. Peacock.

✔ We have ***included*** the new editions of three texts that appeared in the last edition:

- Babbie, E.R. (1995). *The practice of social research* (7th ed.). Belmont, CA: Wadsworth.

- Royse, D.D. [1995]. *Research methods in social work* (2nd ed.). Chicago, IL: Nelson-Hall.

- Yegidis, B.L. & Weinbach, R.W. (1996). *Research methods for social workers* (2nd ed.). Boston, MA: Allyn & Bacon.

ACKNOWLEDGMENTS

WE WISH TO EXPRESS our sincere appreciation to our deans, Frank B. Raymond, III of the University of South Carolina and Ray J. Thomlison of The University of Calgary for their continued support of our efforts. We thank Karen Hanson, Judy Fifer, Jennifer Jacobson, Joyce Nilsen, Catherine Hetmansky, and Marjorie Payne at Allyn and Bacon for their encouragement and guidance.

Marj Andrukow, Denise Ashurst, Peggy Chan, Elsie Johnson, and Jong Won Min made valuable technical contributions and their efforts are appreciated.

We are grateful to the editors of *Arete* and the University of South Carolina, College of Social Work for permission to reprint the five research studies included on pages 130-179:

> **Research Study A:** Victimization of the Elderly: Individual and Family Characteristics of Financial Abuse *by* Jeffery A. Giordano, Bonnie L. Yegidis, and Nan Hervig Giordano (*Arete, 17*, 1992, 26-37).

> **Research Study B**: Does the Social Work Profession Value Research Based Knowledge as a Basis For Social Policy? *by* Beth Spenciner Rosenthal (*Arete, 17*, 1992, 38-47).

> **Research Study C**: Decimating General Assistance: Its Impact on the Relationship of the Poor *by* Anthony P. Halter (*Arete, 17*, 1992, 28-37).

> **Research Study D**: Sexual Adjustment Following Spinal Cord Injury: Empirical Findings and Clinical Implications *by* Romel W. Mackelprang and Dean H. Hepworth (*Arete, 15*, 1990, 1-13).

> **Research Study E**: The Eligibility Worker Role in Public Welfare: Worker and Client Perceptions *by* Nancy P. Kroph, Elizabeth W. Lindsey, and Susan Carse-McLocklin (*Arete, 18*, 1993, 34-42).

Most importantly, we thank the students who use this *Workbook*. We hope that its small purchase price will be justified by an increased understanding and appreciation of the role of research in professional social work practice.

ROBERT W. WEINBACH
RICHARD M. GRINNELL, JR.

Part I
Study Questions

Name:_____

Unit 1
Sources of Knowledge

Social workers rely upon many ways of obtaining knowledge to help guide their practice. They range from tradition, authority, and practice wisdom on one end of the continuum (not scientific) to the use of research findings generated by the scientific method at the other end (very scientific).

Anastas, J.W. & MacDonald, M.L. (1994). *Research design for social work and the human services.* New York: Lexington. **3-22**

Babbie, E.R. (1995). *The practice of social research* (7th ed.). Belmont, CA: Wadsworth. **17-62**

Bailey, K.D. (1994). *Methods of social research* (4th ed.). New York: Free Press. **2-19, 474-485**

DePoy, E. & Gitlin, L.N. (1994). *Introduction to research.* St. Louis, MO: Mosby. **3-14, 28-39**

Frankfort-Nachmias, C. & Nachmias, D. (1992). *Research methods in the social sciences* (4th ed.). New York: St. Martin's Press. **3-50**

Grinnell, R.M., Jr. (Ed.) (1993). *Social work research and evaluation* (4th ed.). Itasca, IL: F.E. Peacock. **2-16**

Judd, C.M., Smith E.R., & Kidder, L.H. (1991). *Research methods in social relations* (6th ed.). Fort Worth, TX: Harcourt Brace Jovanovich. **3-27**

Leedy, P.D. (1993). *Practical research* (5th ed.). New York: Macmillan. **7-24, 109-114**

Marlow, C. (1993). *Research methods for generalist social work.* Pacific Grove, CA: Brooks/Cole. **3-21, 277-293**

Monette, D.R., Sullivan, T.J., & DeJong, C.R. (1994). *Applied social research* (3rd ed.). Fort Worth, TX: Harcourt Brace. **1-30**

Neuman, W.L. (1994). *Social research methods* (2nd ed.). Boston, MA: Allyn & Bacon. **1-16**

Royse, D.D. (1995). *Research methods in social work* (2nd ed.). Chicago, IL: Nelson-Hall. **1-15, 42-43**

Rubin, A. & Babbie, E. (1993). *Research methods for social work* (2nd ed.). Pacific Grove, CA: Brooks/Cole. **2-55, 91-93**

Singleton, R.A., Jr., Straits, B.C., & Miller Straits, M. (1993). *Approaches to social research* (2nd ed.). New York: Oxford. **3-60, 94-96**

Williams, M., Tutty, L.M., & Grinnell, R.M., Jr. (1995). *Research in social work* (2nd ed.). Itasca, IL: F.E. Peacock. **3-30**

Yegidis, B.L. & Weinbach, R.W. (1996). *Research methods for social workers* (2nd ed). Boston, MA: Allyn & Bacon. **3-20**

STUDY QUESTIONS: Answer the following ten questions in the space provided below each question. Use material from your textbook, class lectures, class presentations, class discussions, and other additional readings as necessary.

1. Briefly discuss the past role of research in social work practice. What obstacles to practice utilization of research knowledge have existed?

2. What are the goals of social work research?

3. What other sources of knowledge (besides scientific inquiry) have people traditionally relied upon?

4. List the advantages and disadvantages of each source that you named in your answer to Question 3.

5. Name at least three characteristics of science that make it different from other ways of acquiring "knowledge."

6. In your own words, describe what each of the characteristics that you named in your answer to Question 5 mean.

7. Do you think that the scientific method is more similar to or more dissimilar to the methods used by social work practitioners? Justify your answer.

8. How is the use of theory related to research studies?

9. What is the first step in the scientific research process? Provide a social work example to illustrate your answer.

10. What is (or should be) the last step in the research process? Justify your answer.

APPLICATION QUESTIONS: Read Research Study A (pages 130-140). Answer the following five questions that relate to this study. Integrate the material from your textbook, class lectures, class presentations, class discussions, and additional readings.

11. In reference to Study A, what are some of the non-scientific sources of "knowledge" that have been used in the past to acquire information about older persons? Describe why these non-scientific sources can be misleading.

12. What concepts and theories are discussed in the report?

13. Is the description of research methods described in the methodology section consistent with the usual steps in the scientific research process? Why or why not?

14. List two of the study's findings that were surprising to you. How do they differ from what non-scientific sources of "knowledge" suggest about financial abuse of the elderly?

15. Do you think that the study has good potential for use by the social work practitioner? Are the implications for intervention practical? Why or why not?

Name:_____

Unit 2
Ethical and Political Issues

There are many ethical and political constraints that serve to influence social work research methods. They relate to the use of human research participants for knowledge building and to the researcher's responsibility to other constituencies as well.

Anastas, J.W. & MacDonald, M.L. (1994). *Research design for social work and the human services.* New York: Lexington. **233-257**

Babbie, E.R. (1995). *The practice of social research* (7th ed.). Belmont, CA: Wadsworth. **447-466**

Bailey, K.D. (1994). *Methods of social research* (4th ed.). New York: Free Press. **454-472, 533-545**

DePoy, E. & Gitlin, L.N. (1994). *Introduction to research.* St. Louis, MO: Mosby. **not covered**

Frankfort-Nachmias, C. & Nachmias, D. (1992). *Research methods in the social sciences* (4th ed.). New York: St. Martin's Press. **73-94**

Grinnell, R.M., Jr. (Ed.) (1993). *Social work research and evaluation* (4th ed.). Itasca, IL: F.E. Peacock. **79-90**

Judd, C.M., Smith E.R., & Kidder, L.H. (1991). *Research methods in social relations* (6th ed.). Fort Worth, TX: Harcourt Brace Jovanovich. **477-528**

Leedy, P.D. (1993). *Practical research* (5th ed). New York: Macmillan. **128-131**

Marlow, C. (1993). *Research methods for generalist social work.* Pacific Grove, CA: Brooks/Cole. **13-14, 40, 58-59, 94-95, 117-120**

Monette, D.R., Sullivan, T.J., & DeJong, C.R. (1994). *Applied social research* (3rd ed.). Fort Worth, TX: Harcourt Brace. **44-67**

Neuman, W.L. (1994). *Social research methods* (2nd ed.). Boston, MA: Allyn & Bacon. **427-459**

Royse, D.D. (1995). *Research methods in social work* (2nd ed.). Chicago, IL: Nelson-Hall. **99-100, 301-317**

Rubin, A. & Babbie, E. (1993). *Research methods for social work* (2nd ed.). Pacific Grove, CA: Brooks/Cole. **56-87**

Singleton, R.A., Jr., Straits, B.C., & Miller Straits, M. (1993). *Approaches to social research* (2nd ed.). New York: Oxford. **474-495**

Williams, M., Tutty, L.M., & Grinnell, R.M., Jr. (1995). *Research in social work* (2nd ed.). Itasca, IL: F.E. Peacock. **30-46**

Yegidis, B.L. & Weinbach, R.W. (1996). *Research methods for social workers* (2nd ed). Boston, MA: Allyn & Bacon. **23-37**

STUDY QUESTIONS: Answer the following ten questions in the space provided below each question. Use material from your textbook, class lectures, class presentations, class discussions, and other additional readings as necessary.

1. List two well-known research studies from the past and describe why today they could be considered unethical in their treatment of research participants.

2. What methods are used today to assure that research participants are *voluntary* participants in a research study?

3. Discuss the difference between assurances of anonymity and confidentiality for research participants.

4. What is the meaning of the ethical principle of "no unnecessary pain and suffering" when applied to human research participants? Provide an example.

5. Is deception of research participants ever necessary and/or ethical? Justify your answer using an example.

6. What are Institutional Review Boards and how do they carry out their functions?

7. Do you think that it is ever ethical to withhold treatment from social work clients for research purposes? Why or why not?

8. What does it mean when we say that a researcher has ethical responsibilities to the "scientific community?" What are some of these responsibilities?

9. What ethical issues can arise when a researcher's work is sponsored by some organization? Provide a hypothetical example in your discussion.

10. How can "politics" create ethical issues in relation to the disclosure of a study's results? Provide a hypothetical example in your discussion.

APPLICATION QUESTIONS: Refer to Research Study A and read Research Study B (pages 130-148). Answer the following five questions that relate to these two studies. Integrate the material from your textbook, class lectures, class presentations, class discussions, and additional readings.

11. Is there anything politically sensitive about the findings in Study B? Explain.

12. Do you think that the researcher of Study B met her ethical obligations to the scientific community through the description of her research methods? Why or why not?

13. If the researchers in Study A had wished to conduct follow-up interviews with some of the victims of financial abuse, what could they have done to assure that the research participants were *voluntary* participants?

14. Could the researchers' have provided assurances of anonymity and confidentiality for the research participants? Explain.

15. Could the follow-up interviews cause any physical or emotional discomfort to the research participants? If so, what could the researchers have done to assure that they would leave the participants no worse than they found them?

Unit 3
Problems and Questions

A researcher begins the research process by identifying a general problem area (that results in part from inadequate knowledge) and then formulates one or more research questions that serve as the general focus for the research study.

Anastas, J.W. & MacDonald, M.L. (1994). *Research design for social work and the human services.* New York: Lexington. **33-41, 47-53**

Babbie, E.R. (1995). *The practice of social research* (7th ed.). Belmont, CA: Wadsworth. **56-60**

Bailey, K.D. (1994). *Methods of social research* (4th ed.). New York: Free Press. **21-36**

DePoy, E. & Gitlin, L.N. (1994). *Introduction to research.* St. Louis, MO: Mosby. **17-19**

Frankfort-Nachmias, C. & Nachmias, D. (1992). *Research methods in the social sciences* (4th ed.). New York: St. Martin's Press. **51-54**

Grinnell, R.M., Jr. (Ed.) (1993). *Social work research and evaluation* (4th ed.). Itasca, IL: F.E. Peacock. **17-33**

Judd, C.M., Smith E.R., & Kidder, L.H. (1991). *Research methods in social relations* (6th ed.). Fort Worth, TX: Harcourt Brace Jovanovich. **20-27**

Leedy, P.D. (1993). *Practical research* (5th ed.). New York: Macmillan. **59-86**

Marlow, C. (1993). *Research methods for generalist social work.* Pacific Grove, CA: Brooks/Cole. **23-45**

Monette, D.R., Sullivan, T.J., & DeJong, C.R. (1994). *Applied social research* (3rd ed.). Fort Worth, TX: Harcourt Brace. **68-76**

Neuman, W.L. (1994). *Social research methods* (2nd ed.). Boston, MA: Allyn & Bacon. **55-78, 108-112**

Royse, D.D. (1995). *Research methods in social work* (2nd ed.). Chicago, IL: Nelson-Hall. **17-45**

Rubin, A. & Babbie, E. (1993). *Research methods for social work* (2nd ed.). Pacific Grove, CA: Brooks/Cole. **88-104**

Singleton, R.A., Jr., Straits, B.C., & Miller Straits, M. (1993). *Approaches to social research* (2nd ed.). New York: Oxford. **67-69, 87-88**

Williams, M., Tutty, L.M., & Grinnell, R.M., Jr. (1995). *Research in social work* (2nd ed.). Itasca, IL: F.E. Peacock. **47-80**

Yegidis, B.L. & Weinbach, R.W. (1996). *Research methods for social workers* (2nd ed). Boston, MA: Allyn & Bacon. **41-53**

STUDY QUESTIONS: Answer the following ten questions in the space provided below each question. Use material from your textbook, class lectures, class presentations, class discussions, and other additional readings as necessary.

1. Describe how the purpose of social work research differs from research in other fields like sociology or anthropology.

2. Name and describe some of the factors that can make a social worker want to do a research study.

3. Why would the problem, "lack of accessible post-adoptive counseling services for adoptive parents," be a more suitable problem for social work research than the problem "lack of knowledge of the long term effects on kidney functioning among patients who take the drug Prozac?"

4. What should be the relationship between a research problem and the research question(s) associated with it?

5. Why would we not study a research question whose answer is already known such as, "People who live in poverty have more health problems than people who do not live in poverty?"

6. How might cost be a factor in determining whether it is feasible to study the research question, "Are welfare recipients who are given automobiles more likely to find employment than those who must use public transportation?"

7. Why would it not be feasible to study the research question, "Are clients diagnosed as having a bi-polar disorder whose medication is discontinued more likely to be hospitalized than those who are allowed to continue their medication?"

8. Why would it not be feasible to tell a group of adolescents that they have been diagnosed HIV-positive, study their reactions, and then later tell them that they had been participants in a research study and that they really do not have the disease?

9. Formulate an otherwise appropriate social work research question that it would be impossible to study because of a lack of access to data. Explain.

10. What should be the relationship between a research question and a research hypothesis? Provide an example.

APPLICATION QUESTIONS: Refer to Research Studies A and B, and read Research Study C (pages 130-158). Answer the following five questions that relate to these three studies. Integrate the material from your textbook, class lectures, class presentations, class discussions, and additional readings.

11. State the general research question addressed in Study C.

12. Do you think that the researchers adequately defined and documented the importance of the research problem in the report of Study C? Why or why not?

13. What are the major knowledge gaps that Study A sought to address?

14. Briefly discuss the significance of the research question in Study A. Do the researchers present a convincing argument for its importance? Why or why not?

15. Briefly discuss the importance of the research question in Study B. Do you think that the study was one of high priority? Why or why not?

Name:_____

Unit 4
Literature Review

Usually early in the research process, a thorough literature review is conducted. It pulls together relevant published knowledge (in the form of journal articles and books) about the research problem and assists the researcher in making decisions about how to conduct the study.

Anastas, J.W. & MacDonald, M.L. (1994). *Research design for social work and the human services.* New York: Lexington. **41-47**

Babbie, E.R. (1995). *The practice of social research* (7th ed.). Belmont, CA: Wadsworth. **106, A2-A11**

Bailey, K.D. (1994). *Methods of social research* (4th ed.). New York: Free Press. **not covered**

DePoy, E. & Gitlin, L.N. (1994). *Introduction to research.* St. Louis, MO: Mosby. **61-75**

Frankfort-Nachmias, C. & Nachmias, D. (1992). *Research methods in the social sciences* (4th ed.). New York: St. Martin's Press. **65-69**

Grinnell, R.M., Jr. (Ed.) (1993). *Social work research and evaluation* (4th ed.). Itasca, IL: F.E. Peacock. **388-426**

Judd, C.M., Smith E.R., & Kidder, L.H. (1991). *Research methods in social relations* (6th ed.). Fort Worth, TX: Harcourt Brace Jovanovich. **458-459**

Leedy, P.D. (1993). *Practical research* (5th ed.). New York: Macmillan. **27-31, 87-107**

Marlow, C. (1993). *Research methods for generalist social work.* Pacific Grove, CA: Brooks/Cole. **34-38**

Monette, D.R., Sullivan, T.J., & DeJong, C.R. (1994). *Applied social research* (3rd ed.). Fort Worth, TX: Harcourt Brace. **76-78, 426-443**

Neuman, W.L. (1994). *Social research methods* (2nd ed.). Boston, MA: Allyn & Bacon. **79-95**

Royse, D.D. (1995). *Research methods in social work* (2nd ed.). Chicago, IL: Nelson-Hall. **20-27, 326-328**

Rubin, A. & Babbie, E. (1993). *Research methods for social work* (2nd ed.). Pacific Grove, CA: Brooks/Cole. **104-106, 570-578**

Singleton, R.A., Jr., Straits, B.C., & Miller Straits, M. (1993). *Approaches to social research* (2nd ed.). New York: Oxford. **505**

Williams, M., Tutty, L.M., & Grinnell, R.M., Jr. (1995). *Research in social work* (2nd ed.). Itasca, IL: F.E. Peacock. **306-307**

Yegidis, B.L. & Weinbach, R.W. (1996). *Research methods for social workers* (2nd ed). Boston, MA: Allyn & Bacon. **55-69**

STUDY QUESTIONS: Answer the following ten questions in the space provided below each question. Use material from your textbook, class lectures, class presentations, class discussions, and other additional readings as necessary.

1. What functions does a literature review perform?

2. Name five sources that are widely used in research literature reviews.

3. Of the sources that you named in your answer to Question 2, which one do you regard as the most useful? Why?

4. Is it ever appropriate to include references from publications outside of the literature of social work in a review of literature for a social work research study? Why or why not?

5. In developing a literature review, what should a researcher do if he/she finds reports of several studies that have conflicting findings? Justify your answer.

6. Name three ways in which a thorough literature review can help save time when doing a research study.

7. List three related areas of the literature (topics) that might be useful to examine in a literature review for a research study that seeks to explain negative community attitudes toward Southeast Asian immigrants.

8. How can a researcher know when "enough" literature has been reviewed for a particular research study?

9. Explain how computers can assist the researcher in conducting a literature review.

10. How can a review of literature help the researcher to formulate and/or refine a research hypothesis or sharpen a research question?

APPLICATION QUESTIONS: Refer to Research Studies A, B, and C, and read Research Study D (pages 130-170). Answer the following five questions that relate to these four studies. Integrate the material from your textbook, class lectures, class presentations, class discussions, and additional readings.

11. What do you think about the use of citations from the 1960s and 1970s in the literature review in the report of Study D? Was it appropriate? Why or why not?

12. In reference to Study D, does the literature review flow logically? Is there an appropriate mixture of citations and the authors' own development of ideas on the topic? Justify your answers.

13. Do you think that the researchers in Study A could have brought more relevant knowledge to bear on their topic? What existing knowledge about other groups might have provided some understanding of financial abuse of the elderly?

14. Do you think the researcher in Study B did a good job of assembling and presenting relevant literature? Did the literature seem to suggest the best way for examining the research question? Explain.

15. Do you think that the long list of citations reported in Study C was a valuable contribution for the reader of the report? Why or why not?

Name:_____

Unit 5
Formulating Hypotheses

Not all research studies contain a hypothesis. When formulated, however, it becomes the primary focus of the study. It is based upon the professional literature and, to a lesser degree, personal observations. It is a statement of what the researcher expects to find.

Anastas, J.W. & MacDonald, M.L. (1994). *Research design for social work and the human services.* New York: Lexington. **471, 482-485**

Babbie, E.R. (1995). *The practice of social research* (7th ed.). Belmont, CA: Wadsworth. **48-55, 75-77**

Bailey, K.D. (1994). *Methods of social research* (4th ed.). New York: Free Press. **43-54**

DePoy, E. & Gitlin, L.N. (1994). *Introduction to research.* St. Louis, MO: Mosby. **34-35, 92-93**

Frankfort-Nachmias, C. & Nachmias, D. (1992). *Research methods in the social sciences* (4th ed.). New York: St. Martin's Press. **51-64**

Grinnell, R.M., Jr. (Ed.) (1993). *Social work research and evaluation* (4th ed.). Itasca, IL: F.E. Peacock. **33-37, 94-95**

Judd, C.M., Smith E.R., & Kidder, L.H. (1991). *Research methods in social relations* (6th ed.). Fort Worth, TX: Harcourt Brace Jovanovich. **22-23, 428-431**

Leedy, P.D. (1993). *Practical research* (5th ed.). New York: Macmillan. **14-15, 75-76**

Marlow, C. (1993). *Research methods for generalist social work.* Pacific Grove, CA: Brooks/Cole. **214-216**

Monette, D.R., Sullivan, T.J., & DeJong, C.R. (1994). *Applied social research* (3rd ed.). Fort Worth, TX: Harcourt Brace. **32-35**

Neuman, W.L. (1994). *Social research methods* (2nd ed.). Boston, MA: Allyn & Bacon. **96-113**

Royse, D.D. (1995). *Research methods in social work* (2nd ed.). Chicago, IL: Nelson-Hall. **18-20**

Rubin, A. & Babbie, E. (1993). *Research methods for social work* (2nd ed.). Pacific Grove, CA: Brooks/Cole. **40-42, 120-124**

Singleton, R.A., Jr., Straits, B.C., & Miller Straits, M. (1993). *Approaches to social research* (2nd ed.). New York: Oxford. **88-93**

Williams, M., Tutty, L.M., & Grinnell, R.M., Jr. (1995). *Research in social work* (2nd ed.). Itasca, IL: F.E. Peacock. **81-98**

Yegidis, B.L. & Weinbach, R.W. (1996). *Research methods for social workers* (2nd ed). Boston, MA: Allyn & Bacon. **71-86**

STUDY QUESTIONS: Answer the following ten questions in the space provided below each question. Use material from your textbook, class lectures, class presentations, class discussions, and other additional readings as necessary.

1. What is the definition of a hypothesis used in your text?

2. How is a hypothesis stated differently from a research question? Provide an example of each one using the same research problem.

3. What term is used to describe a characteristic that reflects different measurements among people or objects? Provide a social work example.

4. What term is used to describe its different measurement categories?

5. What do we call the number of times that a particular measurement category occurs within cases studied?

6. How are the terms "independent" and "dependent" (or "predictor" and "criterion") used to clarify the meaning of a directional hypothesis?

7. Create a hypothesis in which one variable is not clearly independent or dependent.

8. What is wrong with the way that the following hypothesis is stated? "Students who study more do better on their examinations than students who do not."

9. Re-state the hypothesis in Question 8 to make it clearer.

10. Make the following statement more testable: "Social workers are good for society."

APPLICATION QUESTIONS: Refer to Research Studies A, B, C, and D, and read Research Study E (pages 130-179). Answer the following five questions that relate to these five studies. Integrate the material from your textbook, class lectures, class presentations, class discussions, and additional readings.

11. Based upon the literature presented and your own practice experiences, re-state the three research questions in Study E as hypotheses.

12. Why did the researchers in Study A use research questions rather than hypotheses? Do you think that they were correct in doing this? Explain.

13. Does the literature review in Study B seem to suggest that one or more hypotheses would have been appropriate? Why or why not?

14. Discuss why you would (or would not) have expected to find hypotheses in Study C. Justify your answer.

15. Based upon their review of literature, formulate two hypotheses that the researchers in Study D could have used. Specify the dependent (criterion) variable in parentheses after each of your hypotheses.

Unit 6
Research Design: General

Every research study employs some form of a research design. It is a plan for collecting and analyzing data that, the researcher hopes, will generate an answer to the research question. Designs are given labels based upon their major characteristics.

Anastas, J.W. & MacDonald, M.L. (1994). *Research design for social work and the human services.* New York: Lexington. **22-32, 53-99, 142-145**

Babbie, E.R. (1995). *The practice of social research* (7th ed.). Belmont, CA: Wadsworth. **83-107**

Bailey, K.D. (1994). *Methods of social research* (4th ed.). New York: Free Press. **15-17, 36-41**

DePoy, E. & Gitlin, L.N. (1994). *Introduction to research.* St. Louis, MO: Mosby. **16-26, 77-85, 146-159**

Frankfort-Nachmias, C. & Nachmias, D. (1992). *Research methods in the social sciences* (4th ed.). New York: St. Martin's Press. **97-99, 271-290**

Grinnell, R.M., Jr. (Ed.) (1993). *Social work research and evaluation* (4th ed.). Itasca, IL: F.E. Peacock. **38-78, 118-119, 262-267**

Judd, C.M., Smith E.R., & Kidder, L.H. (1991). *Research methods in social relations* (6th ed.). Fort Worth, TX: Harcourt Brace Jovanovich. **27-36, 298-320**

Leedy, P.D. (1993). *Practical research* (5th ed). New York: Macmillan. **113-128, 137-147**

Marlow, C. (1993). *Research methods for generalist social work.* Pacific Grove, CA: Brooks/Cole. **23-27, 66-68, 95-96, 137-138**

Monette, D.R., Sullivan, T.J., & DeJong, C.R. (1994). *Applied social research* (3rd ed.). Fort Worth, TX: Harcourt Brace. **82-92**

Neuman, W.L. (1994). *Social research methods* (2nd ed.). Boston, MA: Allyn & Bacon. **55-78**

Royse, D.D. (1995). *Research methods in social work* (2nd ed.). Chicago, IL: Nelson-Hall. **27-30, 79-100**

Rubin, A. & Babbie, E. (1993). *Research methods for social work* (2nd ed.). Pacific Grove, CA: Brooks/Cole. **29-30, 106-112, 357-365**

Singleton, R.A., Jr., Straits, B.C., & Miller Straits, M. (1993). *Approaches to social research* (2nd ed.). New York: Oxford. **67-87, 91-96**

Williams, M., Tutty, L.M., & Grinnell, R.M., Jr. (1995). *Research in social work* (2nd ed.). Itasca, IL: F.E. Peacock. **195-222**

Yegidis, B.L. & Weinbach, R.W. (1996). *Research methods for social workers* (2nd ed). Boston, MA: Allyn & Bacon. **89-111**

STUDY QUESTIONS: Answer the following ten questions in the space provided below each question. Use material from your textbook, class lectures, class presentations, class discussions, and other additional readings as necessary.

1. When we know very little about a research problem, what type of research designs are generally used? What is their primary purpose?

2. Which type of research design would be best to attempt to document the extent of a problem, such as the difficulties faced by homeless people in Los Angeles?

3. How can the results of the research study that you mentioned in your answer to Question 2 be of benefit to the social work practitioner?

4. What general type of research study seeks to explain why something happens, e.g, why some employees choose not to use needed counseling services offered at no charge to them through their Employment Assistance Plan? What knowledge can it produce that the other types of research studies cannot?

5. Sometimes research studies may have more than one purpose. They combine elements of different types of research designs. Is this ever desirable? Explain.

6. What are longitudinal research studies and what can they tell us that more traditional cross-sectional research studies cannot?

7. In what ways do the different types of longitudinal research studies differ? Provide an example of each one.

8. What does it mean when we say that qualitative (or naturalistic) research is more inductive while quantitative (or positivistic) research is more deductive?

9. What is the place of hypotheses in qualitative research studies? How do they differ from their place in quantitative research studies?

10. What are some of the characteristics of "feminist research?"

APPLICATION QUESTIONS: Refer to Research Studies A, B, C, D, and E (pages 130-179). Answer the following five questions that relate to these five studies. Integrate the material from your textbook, class lectures, class presentations, class discussions, and additional readings.

11. Study A employed a research design that was primarily descriptive. What did the researchers seek to describe? How might their descriptive findings be of value to the social work practitioner?

12. What design label(s) should be used to discuss the basic methods employed by the researcher in Study B? Was this design consistent with the research question? Explain.

13. Did the qualitative research methods employed by the researchers in Study C help them to understand how persons denied financial assistance experienced this problem? Was the use of direct quotations helpful in this regard? Why or why not?

14. Briefly discuss how the research problem in Study D could have been studied using a longitudinal research design? What would the data from such a design tell the researchers that the design described in the research report did not?

15. What research design was used in Study E? Was the implications section of the report consistent with what you would expect to find for this type of research design? Why or why not?

Name:_____

Unit 7
Survey Research

Surveys remain an important form of data collection. They are used to describe a wide variety of conditions and problems. They are effective and efficient ways of collecting large amounts of data. But, like all forms of research designs, they also have limitations.

Anastas, J.W. & MacDonald, M.L. (1994). *Research design for social work and the human services.* New York: Lexington. **100-125**

Babbie, E.R. (1995). *The practice of social research* (7th ed.). Belmont, CA: Wadsworth. **256-277**

Bailey, K.D. (1994). *Methods of social research* (4th ed.). New York: Free Press. **148-172, 196-208**

DePoy, E. & Gitlin, L.N. (1994). *Introduction to research.* St. Louis, MO: Mosby. **117**

Frankfort-Nachmias, C. & Nachmias, D. (1992). *Research methods in the social sciences* (4th ed.). New York: St. Martin's Press. **215-237**

Grinnell, R.M., Jr. (Ed.) (1993). *Social work research and evaluation* (4th ed.). Itasca, IL: F.E. Peacock. **262-289**

Judd, C.M., Smith E.R., & Kidder, L.H. (1991). *Research methods in social relations* (6th ed.). Fort Worth, TX: Harcourt Brace Jovanovich. **100-127, 213-227**

Leedy, P.D. (1993). *Practical research* (5th ed.). New York: Macmillan. **185-195, 213-216**

Marlow, C. (1993). *Research methods for generalist social work.* Pacific Grove, CA: Brooks/Cole. **65-77**

Monette, D.R., Sullivan, T.J., & DeJong, C.R. (1994). *Applied social research* (3rd ed.). Fort Worth, TX: Harcourt Brace. **153-186**

Neuman, W.L. (1994). *Social research methods* (2nd ed.). Boston, MA: Allyn & Bacon. **221-258**

Royse, D.D. (1995). *Research methods in social work* (2nd ed.). Chicago, IL: Nelson-Hall. **145-175, 214-217**

Rubin, A. & Babbie, E. (1993). *Research methods for social work* (2nd ed.). Pacific Grove, CA: Brooks/Cole. **332-356**

Singleton, R.A., Jr., Straits, B.C., & Miller Straits, M. (1993). *Approaches to social research* (2nd ed.). New York: Oxford. **246-279**

Williams, M., Tutty, L.M., & Grinnell, R.M., Jr. (1995). *Research in social work* (2nd ed.). Itasca, IL: F.E. Peacock. **239-260**

Yegidis, B.L. & Weinbach, R.W. (1996). *Research methods for social workers* (2nd ed). Boston, MA: Allyn & Bacon. **172-194**

STUDY QUESTIONS: Answer the following ten questions in the space provided below each question. Use material from your textbook, class lectures, class presentations, class discussions, and other additional readings as necessary.

1. What are the advantages and disadvantages of using standardized data collection instruments in survey research studies?

2. Why should a self-administered questionnaire always be pilot-tested before actual research data are collected? What is examined when it is pilot-tested? Provide an example.

3. Name at least three limitations in the use of mailed, self-administered question-naires and describe their limitations.

4. Name at least five things a researcher can do to attempt to increase the response rate when using mailed, self-administered questionnaires for data collection.

5. How have recent technological advances in the telephone industry presented both advantages and disadvantages for researchers wishing to conduct telephone surveys?

6. Give several reasons why it would not be feasible to conduct a mailed, survey of persons with AIDS who use no precautions to prevent others from getting the disease.

7. If literacy of respondents is likely to be a problem, what method(s) of data collection can be used? Explain your response in detail.

8. What are the major strengths and limitations of telephone surveys?

9. What are the advantages and disadvantages of using in-person interviews to conduct surveys?

10. Why are in-person interviews generally regarded as the most expensive form of data collection method used in survey research?

APPLICATION QUESTIONS: Refer to Research Studies A, B, C, D, and E (pages 130-179). Answer the following five questions that relate to these five studies. Integrate the material from your textbook, class lectures, class presentations, class discussions, and additional readings.

11. Briefly describe why it would not be possible to conduct a good telephone survey of the victims of financial abuse that were described in Study A.

12. If a mailed questionnaire survey were to be used to examine the research question in Study B, who would be a good choice for research participants to receive the survey? Explain.

13. Describe briefly how a mailed survey has been used to gather data to answer the research questions in Study C. What would be the major disadvantages of using this method of data collection?

14. What would be the major advantages and disadvantages of using in-person interviews to study the research question in Study D?

15. Why do you think that the researchers described the response rate of 68% as "high" for clients in Study E, given what you know about mailed surveys and about the research participants? Explain.

Unit 8
Correlation and Causality

Both descriptive and explanatory research studies generally allow the researcher to demonstrate relationships between and among variables. But the nature of the relationships that can be claimed are very different depending on the specific design utilized.

Anastas, J.W. & MacDonald, M.L. (1994). *Research design for social work and the human services.* New York: Lexington. **128-196**

Babbie, E.R. (1995). *The practice of social research* (7th ed.). Belmont, CA: Wadsworth. **233-253**

Bailey, K.D. (1994). *Methods of social research* (4th ed.). New York: Free Press. **48-50, 218-239**

DePoy, E. & Gitlin, L.N. (1994). *Introduction to research.* St. Louis, MO: Mosby. **87-95, 102-116**

Frankfort-Nachmias, C. & Nachmias, D. (1992). *Research methods in the social sciences* (4th ed.). New York: St. Martin's Press. **100-146**

Grinnell, R.M., Jr. (Ed.) (1993). *Social work research and evaluation* (4th ed.). Itasca, IL: F.E. Peacock. **118-153**

Judd, C.M., Smith E.R., & Kidder, L.H. (1991). *Research methods in social relations* (6th ed.). Fort Worth, TX: Harcourt Brace Jovanovich. **68-127**

Leedy, P.D. (1993). *Practical research* (5th ed.). New York: Macmillan. **274-278, 295-311**

Marlow, C. (1993). *Research methods for generalist social work.* Pacific Grove, CA: Brooks/Cole. **125-149**

Monette, D.R., Sullivan, T.J., & DeJong, C.R. (1994). *Applied social research* (3rd ed.). Fort Worth, TX: Harcourt Brace. **247-281**

Neuman, W.L. (1994). *Social research methods* (2nd ed.). Boston, MA: Allyn & Bacon. **169-192**

Royse, D.D. (1995). *Research methods in social work* (2nd ed.). Chicago, IL: Nelson-Hall. **79-100**

Rubin, A. & Babbie, E. (1993). *Research methods for social work* (2nd ed.). Pacific Grove, CA: Brooks/Cole. **261-291**

Singleton, R.A., Jr., Straits, B.C., & Miller Straits, M. (1993). *Approaches to social research* (2nd ed.). New York: Oxford. **80-87, 181-242**

Williams, M., Tutty, L.M., & Grinnell, R.M., Jr. (1995). *Research in social work* (2nd ed.). Itasca, IL: F.E. Peacock. **133-160**

Yegidis, B.L. & Weinbach, R.W. (1996). *Research methods for social workers* (2nd ed). Boston, MA: Allyn & Bacon. **95-103**

STUDY QUESTIONS: Answer the following ten questions in the space provided below each question. Use material from your textbook, class lectures, class presentations, class discussions, and other additional readings as necessary.

1. What does it mean when a research study has found evidence for an association between the gender of social workers and their client success rate? What does it *not* mean?

2. What does it mean when a research study has found evidence for a negative correlation between age and assertiveness among social work students? What does it *not* mean?

3. Name three other possible explanations (rival hypotheses) besides a cause-effect relationship for the apparent relationship between the gender of social workers and their client success rate described in Question 1.

4. What is a "quasi-experimental" research design and how does it differ from a true experiment? Provide a social work research example of both types of designs?

5. What function does randomization perform in research designs?

6. What is the main purpose of using one or more control groups in a true experiment?

7. Discuss the advantages and disadvantages of using a pretest measurement of the dependent variable when conducting a research study.

8. The findings of an experiment demonstrated that one treatment worked better than another with an agency's clinically depressed clients. But it was concluded that the finding lacked external validity. What does this mean?

9. In reference to Question 8, what would it mean if it was stated that the study lacked internal validity?

10. Name two threats to internal validity that may have been operating in the study described in Question 8. Describe how they might have influenced the results of the study.

APPLICATION QUESTIONS: Refer to Research Studies A, C, D, and E (pages 130-140, 149-179). Answer the following five questions that relate to these four studies. Integrate the material from your textbook, class lectures, class presentations, class discussions, and additional readings.

11. In reference to Study A, do you agree with what the authors conclude about the external validity of their findings in the limitations section in the report? Why or why not?

12. In reference to Study C, name five possible other reasons for some of the changes in the lives of the former clients (besides loss of welfare benefits).

13. In reference to Study C, why would it be impossible to conclude on the basis that denial of welfare benefits produces poorer relationships with friends or relatives? How could the use of a control group have helped? Who would have constituted such a group?

14. In reference to Study D, why would it have been both ethically and logistically unfeasible to have studied the research problem using a true experimental design?

15. In reference to Study E, why would the study's findings probably have little external validity?

Name:_____

Unit 9
Secondary Data Analysis

Many research questions can be answered and hypotheses tested using data that already are available because they were gathered for some other purpose. This can be a time- and cost-saver for the researcher but the secondary analysis of existing data also has its limitations.

Anastas, J.W. & MacDonald, M.L. (1994). *Research design for social work and the human services*. New York: Lexington. **not covered**

Babbie, E.R. (1995). *The practice of social research* (7th ed.). Belmont, CA: Wadsworth. **274-276, 321-335**

Bailey, K.D. (1994). *Methods of social research* (4th ed.). New York: Free Press. **294-319, 410-412**

DePoy, E. & Gitlin, L.N. (1994). *Introduction to research*. St. Louis, MO: Mosby. **192-193, 223-225**

Frankfort-Nachmias, C. & Nachmias, D. (1992). *Research methods in the social sciences* (4th ed.). New York: St. Martin's Press. **291-318**

Grinnell, R.M., Jr. (Ed.) (1993). *Social work research and evaluation* (4th ed.). Itasca, IL: F.E. Peacock. **290-303, 367-385**

Judd, C.M., Smith E.R., & Kidder, L.H. (1991). *Research methods in social relations* (6th ed.). Fort Worth, TX: Harcourt Brace Jovanovich. **287-296, 425-449**

Leedy, P.D. (1993). *Practical research* (5th ed.). New York: Macmillan. **223-239**

Marlow, C. (1993). *Research methods for generalist social work*. Pacific Grove, CA: Brooks/Cole. **81-83, 237**

Monette, D.R., Sullivan, T.J., & DeJong, C.R. (1994). *Applied social research* (3rd ed.). Fort Worth, TX: Harcourt Brace. **187-212**

Neuman, W.L. (1994). *Social research methods* (2nd ed.). Boston, MA: Allyn & Bacon. **81, 261-278**

Royse, D.D. (1995). *Research methods in social work* (2nd ed.). Chicago, IL: Nelson-Hall. **206-227**

Rubin, A. & Babbie, E. (1993). *Research methods for social work* (2nd ed.). Pacific Grove, CA: Brooks/Cole. **404-431, 499-501**

Singleton, R.A., Jr., Straits, B.C., & Miller Straits, M. (1993). *Approaches to social research* (2nd ed.). New York: Oxford. **251-252, 354-388**

Williams, M., Tutty, L.M., & Grinnell, R.M., Jr. (1995). *Research in social work* (2nd ed.). Itasca, IL: F.E. Peacock. **261-276**

Yegidis, B.L. & Weinbach, R.W. (1996). *Research methods for social workers* (2nd ed). Boston, MA: Allyn & Bacon. **159-164**

STUDY QUESTIONS: Answer the following ten questions in the space provided below each question. Use material from your textbook, class lectures, class presentations, class discussions, and other additional readings as necessary.

1. How has the development of data archives and computerization made secondary analysis of data more possible? Provide an example.

2. What are some of the most common sources of secondary data available to social workers?

3. What are some of the advantages and disadvantages of using agency records as data sources for social work research studies?

4. Using personal statements from student BSW admission applications, a researcher hopes to learn the answer to the question, "Are male social workers more interested in administration than female social workers?" List several potential problems that you see in using this method of secondary analysis to answer the research question.

5. What would be a better source of secondary data to use to attempt to answer the research question stated in Question 4? Why would it be better?

6. Why might it be necessary to collect original data to study the research question in Question 4? Why would any secondary data source present problems for the researcher?

7. What forms of secondary data does content analysis examine? Provide a social work example of each one.

8. Why is are content analyses often time consuming? Provide an example to support your answer.

9. What is the purpose of historical research? How can it be used by social workers to address present problems? Provide an example.

10. In your own words, briefly describe what meta-analysis is and how it is conducted.

APPLICATION QUESTIONS: Refer to Research Studies A and B (pages 130-148). Answer the following five questions that relate to these two studies. Integrate the material from your textbook, class lectures, class presentations, class discussions, and additional readings.

11. Study A relied on secondary analysis of data taken from case records. What was the original purpose for which the data were collected?

12. In reference to Study A, the researchers briefly mention possible limitations of their use of case record data. What are some other ways in which the use of existing data may have weakened their ability to study the research questions?

13. Study B relied on content analysis to study a research question. What form of communication was the source for the researchers' data? What is the usual purpose for this communication? How might this affect the researcher's data? Explain.

14. What are some of the limitations of the data used in Study B and how might they have biased the researcher's findings?

15. What other secondary sources might have been used for data for studying the research question in Study B? Discuss how these data might have been used to provide either support or non-support for the study's findings.

Unit 10
Single-Subject Research

Social workers need simple methods to determine if their interventions are effective. Single-subject research designs provide them with a means to assess whether their methods of intervention seem to be making a difference in their work with various client systems.

Anastas, J.W. & MacDonald, M.L. (1994). *Research design for social work and the human services.* New York: Lexington. **197-230**

Babbie, E.R. (1995). *The practice of social research* (7th ed.). Belmont, CA: Wadsworth. **not covered**

Bailey, K.D. (1994). *Methods of social research* (4th ed.). New York: Free Press. **not covered**

DePoy, E. & Gitlin, L.N. (1994). *Introduction to research.* St. Louis, MO: Mosby. **113-114**

Frankfort-Nachmias, C. & Nachmias, D. (1992). *Research methods in the social sciences* (4th ed.). New York: St. Martin's Press. **not covered**

Grinnell, R.M., Jr. (Ed.) (1993). *Social work research and evaluation* (4th ed.). Itasca, IL: F.E. Peacock. **94-117**

Judd, C.M., Smith E.R., & Kidder, L.H. (1991). *Research methods in social relations* (6th ed.). Fort Worth, TX: Harcourt Brace Jovanovich. **not covered**

Leedy, P.D. (1993). *Practical research: Planning and design* (5th ed.). New York: Macmillan. **not covered**

Marlow, C. (1993). *Research methods for generalist social work.* Pacific Grove, CA: Brooks/Cole. **29, 151-173**

Monette, D.R., Sullivan, T.J., & DeJong, C.R. (1994). *Applied social research* (3rd ed.). Fort Worth, TX: Harcourt Brace. **282-311**

Neuman, W.L. (1994). *Social research methods* (2nd ed.). Boston, MA: Allyn & Bacon. **not covered**

Royse, D.D. (1995). *Research methods in social work* (2nd ed.). Chicago, IL: Nelson-Hall. **49-72**

Rubin, A. & Babbie, E. (1993). *Research methods for social work* (2nd ed.). Pacific Grove, CA: Brooks/Cole. **292-328**

Singleton, R.A., Jr., Straits, B.C., & Miller Straits, M. (1993). *Approaches to social research* (2nd ed.). New York: Oxford. **not covered**

Williams, M., Tutty, L.M., & Grinnell, R.M., Jr. (1995). *Research in social work* (2nd ed.). Itasca, IL: F.E. Peacock. **161-194**

Yegidis, B.L. & Weinbach, R.W. (1996). *Research methods for social workers* (2nd ed). Boston, MA: Allyn & Bacon. **233-255**

STUDY QUESTIONS: Answer the following ten questions in the space provided below each question. Use material from your textbook, class lectures, class presentations, class discussions, and other additional readings as necessary.

1. What is the dependent (criterion) variable in single-subject research? Provide a social work example of one.

2. What is the independent (predictor) variable in single-subject research? Provide a social work example of one.

3. What are the *A* and *B* phases and how do they differ? Provide a social work example of how they could be used in a practice situation.

4. What are the different ways that a researcher can measure a target behavior (target problem) such as a child's tendency to throw tantrums in public places? Explain.

5. What is the purpose of using more than one *A* phase in a single-subject research study?

6. A client does not abuse alcohol while being treated for alcohol abuse. However, the client abuses it when the treatment is withdrawn. Does this mean that the treatment is successful? Explain your answer.

7. Discuss the external validity of single-subject research designs. How can they be used to produce generalized knowledge for social work practice?

8. In what type of situation might the basic *AB* design be appropriate? Provide a social work example of an *AB* design.

9. Briefly discuss the ethical issues involved in a single-subject research design that begins with an *A* phase.

10. Is single-subject research true research, just good practice, or both? Justify your opinion by providing a social work example throughout your discussion.

APPLICATION QUESTIONS: Refer to Research Studies C and D (pages 149-170). Answer the following five questions that relate to these two studies. Integrate the material from your textbook, class lectures, class presentations, class discussions, and additional readings.

11. Suppose that you are providing counseling services to one of the former general assistance clients who was a research participant in Study C. What might be an appropriate target behavior to use in conducting single-subject research to evaluate your effectiveness in working with the client? Would you measure its frequency, interval, duration, or magnitude? Explain why.

12. In reference to Study C, specify an intervention or treatment that you could use in your study while continuing to offer the usual services to the client.

13. With reference to Questions 11 and 12, would you begin with an *A* or a *B* phase? Why?

14. Suppose that you are providing counseling services to one of the individuals who suffered spinal cord injury who was a research participant in Study D. Specify a target behavior that you might seek to increase (frequency) and an intervention that you might use to try to increase it. How could you test the effectiveness of the intervention using a single-subject research design?

15. In relation to Question 14, suppose the target behavior was found to increase rapidly during the *B* phases of your research study and to decrease rapidly during the *A* phases. Would this indicate treatment effectiveness? Why or why not? Be sure to address the issue of dependency.

Unit 11
Evaluation Research

Evaluation research designs (sometimes called program evaluation) are used to evaluate the effectiveness of present and potential social work programs. They entail a wide variety of research designs, data-collection strategies, and foci.

Anastas, J.W. & MacDonald, M.L. (1994). *Research design for social work and the human services.* New York: Lexington. **not covered**

Babbie, E.R. (1995). *The practice of social research* (7th ed.). Belmont, CA: Wadsworth. **338-358**

Bailey, K.D. (1994). *Methods of social research* (4th ed.). New York: Free Press. **486-490**

DePoy, E. & Gitlin, L.N. (1994). *Introduction to research.* St. Louis, MO: Mosby. **not covered**

Frankfort-Nachmias, C. & Nachmias, D. (1992). *Research methods in the social sciences* (4th ed.). New York: St. Martin's Press. **not covered**

Grinnell, R.M., Jr. (Ed.) (1993). *Social work research and evaluation* (4th ed.). Itasca, IL: F.E. Peacock. **not covered**

Judd, C.M., Smith E.R., & Kidder, L.H. (1991). *Research methods in social relations* (6th ed.). Fort Worth, TX: Harcourt Brace Jovanovich. **321-349**

Leedy, P.D. (1993). *Practical research* (5th ed.). New York: Macmillan. **not covered**

Marlow, C. (1993). *Research methods for generalist social work.* Pacific Grove, CA: Brooks/Cole. **30-34**

Monette, D.R., Sullivan, T.J., & DeJong, C.R. (1994). *Applied social research* (3rd ed.). Fort Worth, TX: Harcourt Brace. **312-339**

Neuman, W.L. (1994). *Social research methods* (2nd ed.). Boston, MA: Allyn & Bacon. **23-26**

Royse, D.D. (1995). *Research methods in social work* (2nd ed.). Chicago, IL: Nelson-Hall. **259-277**

Rubin, A. & Babbie, E. (1993). *Research methods for social work* (2nd ed.). Pacific Grove, CA: Brooks/Cole. **536-568**

Singleton, R.A., Jr., Straits, B.C., & Miller Straits, M. (1993). *Approaches to social research* (2nd ed.). New York: Oxford. **238-241**

Williams, M., Tutty, L.M., & Grinnell, R.M., Jr. (1995). *Research in social work* (2nd ed.). Itasca, IL: F.E. Peacock. **not covered**

Yegidis, B.L. & Weinbach, R.W. (1996). *Research methods for social workers* (2nd ed). Boston, MA: Allyn & Bacon. **215-230**

STUDY QUESTIONS: Answer the following ten questions in the space provided below each question. Use material from your textbook, class lectures, class presentations, class discussions, and other additional readings as necessary.

1. How has an increased emphasis on accountability in recent times contributed to a greater emphasis on evaluative research?

2. What do we call the form of evaluation research that determines if a program is needed and/or should be offered? Provide an example of this type of research study.

3. In reference to Question 2, what other types of questions does this type of evaluative research address?

4. What kind of questions are asked in program evaluations that examine program implementation?

5. What kind of evaluation focuses on program outcome? Provide a social work example of one.

6. Define program efficiency and effectiveness and describe how they are related in the context of evaluation research.

7. What is cost-benefit analysis and what are some of the problems in using it to evaluate a social program?

8. Describe how a qualitative approach to program evaluation might differ from a quantitative one.

9. What are the advantages and disadvantages of using program evaluators who are not employees of the organization being evaluated?

10. Describe how "politics" can represent a threat to an objective program evaluation. Use an example in your discussion.

APPLICATION QUESTIONS: Refer to Research Studies A and E (pages 130-140, 171-179). Answer the following five questions that relate to these two studies. Integrate the material from your textbook, class lectures, class presentations, class discussions, and additional readings.

11. Suppose that a social agency that serves older clients is considering offering a program of counseling and support services to victims of financial abuse such as those described in Study A. Briefly describe what types of questions the agency administrator might want to answer in a needs assessment designed to help in planning for the program.

12. In reference to Study A, list several sources and groups of people that would provide data for the need assessment.

13. In reference to Study A, if the program were to be implemented, what type of questions would a program evaluation study ask six months after the program has begun?

14. What program did Study E attempt to evaluate? What type of evaluation was used? How would the questions asked by this type of evaluation differ from those that would be asked in the one described in Question 13?

15. In reference to Study E, do you think that the implications for the training of public assistance workers were supported by the study's findings? Why or why not?

Unit 12
Sampling

Generally, it is impractical to study all persons or objects of interest. Thus, a researcher selects a small number of persons or objects (a sample) from a population to represent the population. There are a number of different ways to obtain a sample.

Anastas, J.W. & MacDonald, M.L. (1994). *Research design for social work and the human services.* New York: Lexington. **258-282**

Babbie, E.R. (1995). *The practice of social research* (7th ed.). Belmont, CA: Wadsworth. **187-226, 310-311**

Bailey, K.D. (1994). *Methods of social research* (4th ed.). New York: Free Press. **82-104**

DePoy, E. & Gitlin, L.N. (1994). *Introduction to research.* St. Louis, MO: Mosby. **163-183**

Frankfort-Nachmias, C. & Nachmias, D. (1992). *Research methods in the social sciences* (4th ed.). New York: St. Martin's Press. **169-193**

Grinnell, R.M., Jr. (Ed.) (1993). *Social work research and evaluation* (4th ed.). Itasca, IL: F.E. Peacock. **154-170**

Judd, C.M., Smith E.R., & Kidder, L.H. (1991). *Research methods in social relations* (6th ed.). Fort Worth, TX: Harcourt Brace Jovanovich. **128-142, 201-212**

Leedy, P.D. (1993). *Practical research* (5th ed.). New York: Macmillan. **197-213**

Marlow, C. (1993). *Research methods for generalist social work.* Pacific Grove, CA: Brooks/Cole. **103-123**

Monette, D.R., Sullivan, T.J., & DeJong, C.R. (1994). *Applied social research* (3rd ed.). Fort Worth, TX: Harcourt Brace. **119-152**

Neuman, W.L. (1994). *Social research methods* (2nd ed.). Boston, MA: Allyn & Bacon. **193-220**

Royse, D.D. (1995). *Research methods in social work* (2nd ed.). Chicago, IL: Nelson-Hall. **157-175**

Rubin, A. & Babbie, E. (1993). *Research methods for social work* (2nd ed.). Pacific Grove, CA: Brooks/Cole. **217-260**

Singleton, R.A., Jr., Straits, B.C., & Miller Straits, M. (1993). *Approaches to social research* (2nd ed.). New York: Oxford. **136-172**

Williams, M., Tutty, L.M., & Grinnell, R.M., Jr. (1995). *Research in social work* (2nd ed.). Itasca, IL: F.E. Peacock. **223-238**

Yegidis, B.L. & Weinbach, R.W. (1996). *Research methods for social workers* (2nd ed). Boston, MA: Allyn & Bacon. **113-125**

STUDY QUESTIONS: Answer the following ten questions in the space provided below each question. Use material from your textbook, class lectures, class presentations, class discussions, and other additional readings as necessary.

1. How does a sample differ from a population? Provide an example of a sample drawn from a population.

2. What is a sampling frame? When is it necessary to use a sampling frame rather than a population to draw a research sample? Provide an example.

3. What are two characteristics used to evaluate the adequacy of a research sample? What does each mean?

4. Why is the absolute number of cases in a sample generally more important than the percentage of the population that the sample represents? Explain.

5. What is sampling error? How does it differ from sampling bias? Provide an example of each one.

6. What is the basic difference between a probability sample and a non-probability sample? Provide a social work example of each type.

7. Which non-probability sampling method is sometimes used to deliberately create a non-representative (atypical) sample that reflects as much diversity as possible? Provide an example of when such a sample might be desirable.

8. What do we call the process for reducing sampling error that entails the grouping of cases into similar subcategories (strata) before sampling?

9. What is the method called that is sometimes used to control for one or more intervening (extraneous) variables while assigning cases to experimental and control groups? Provide an example of how this might be done.

10. In what situations would obtaining a sample be unnecessary? Justify your answer and provide a social work example in your response.

APPLICATION QUESTIONS: Refer to Research Studies A, B, C, D, and E (pages 130-179). Answer the following five questions that relate to these five studies. Integrate the material from your textbook, class lectures, class presentations, class discussions, and additional readings.

11. Why might the research subjects in Study A not be a representative sample of elderly victims of financial abuse? What older victims were systematically eliminated from their sample because of the sampling frame used?

12. Was sampling employed in Study B? Explain.

13. Why would the research participants in Study C not be considered a representative sample of persons who experienced discontinuance of general financial assistance? How does this limit the value of the study's findings?

14. Evaluate the size and representativeness of the research sample used in Study D. How might the loss of 34 spinal cord injury participants from the initial sampling frame have biased the sample of persons from whom data were collected? Explain.

15. Why do the researchers in Study E suggest in the limitations section of the report that their sample of responses from clients may have been biased? What do researchers call this type of biasing effect?

Unit 13
Measurement

Measurement refers to the methods used by the researcher to sort cases into the appropriate categories (values) of a variable. Without good measurement of variables, it is impossible to draw accurate conclusions about the relationships between and among variables.

Anastas, J.W. & MacDonald, M.L. (1994). *Research design for social work and the human services*. New York: Lexington. **283-314, 432-439**

Babbie, E.R. (1995). *The practice of social research* (7th ed.). Belmont, CA: Wadsworth. **110-139**

Bailey, K.D. (1994). *Methods of social research* (4th ed.). New York: Free Press. **62-77**

DePoy, E. & Gitlin, L.N. (1994). *Introduction to research*. St. Louis, MO: Mosby. **194-209**

Frankfort-Nachmias, C. & Nachmias, D. (1992). *Research methods in the social sciences* (4th ed.). New York: St. Martin's Press. **30-34, 147-168**

Grinnell, R.M., Jr. (Ed.) (1993). *Social work research and evaluation* (4th ed.). Itasca, IL: F.E. Peacock. **174-197**

Judd, C.M., Smith E.R., & Kidder, L.H. (1991). *Research methods in social relations* (6th ed.). Fort Worth, TX: Harcourt Brace Jovanovich. **41-67**

Leedy, P.D. (1993). *Practical research* (5th ed.). New York: Macmillan. **31-42, 213-215**

Marlow, C. (1993). *Research methods for generalist social work*. Pacific Grove, CA: Brooks/Cole. **47-63**

Monette, D.R., Sullivan, T.J., & DeJong, C.R. (1994). *Applied social research* (3rd ed.). Fort Worth, TX: Harcourt Brace. **93-118**

Neuman, W.L. (1994). *Social research methods* (2nd ed.). Needham Heights, MA: Allyn& Bacon. **120-144**

Royse, D.D. (1995). *Research methods in social work* (2nd ed.). Chicago, IL: Nelson-Hall. **106-112, 241-243**

Rubin, A. & Babbie, E. (1993). *Research methods for social work* (2nd ed.). Pacific Grove, CA: Brooks/Cole. **119-181**

Singleton, R.A., Jr., Straits, B.C., & Miller Straits, M. (1993). *Approaches to social research* (2nd ed.). New York: Oxford. **100-130**

Williams, M., Tutty, L.M., & Grinnell, R.M., Jr. (1995). *Research in social work* (2nd ed.). Itasca, IL: F.E. Peacock. **99-114**

Yegidis, B.L. & Weinbach, R.W. (1996). *Research methods for social workers* (2nd ed). Needham Heights, MA: Allyn & Bacon. **125-136**

STUDY QUESTIONS: Answer the following ten questions in the space provided below each question. Use material from your textbook, class lectures, class presentations, class discussions, and other additional readings as necessary.

1. Conceptualization is the first step in the measurement process. What is conceptualization? Provide an example of how it is used in the research process.

2. Once variables have been conceptualized, they must be operationalized? What does this mean? Provide an example.

3. What are three different ways that a researcher might operationalize the variable "assertiveness?"

4. What do the labels nominal, ordinal, interval, and ratio refer to in describing the measurement of a variable? Provide an example of each one.

5. Explain how the way that a variable is operationalized can affect the level of measurement of the variable. Provide an example.

6. What is the difference between reliability and validity in measurement and how do they relate to each other?

7. Briefly describe two methods for establishing reliability and mention a research situation where each would be important.

8. What is the difference between concurrent validity and predictive validity? When would each type be especially important to the researcher?

9. If a question on an examination in this course asked you the name of the author of your textbook, why could you argue that the question lacks content validity?

10. Briefly describe several types of errors that occur in the measurement of variables.

APPLICATION QUESTIONS: Refer to Research Studies A, B, C, D, and E (pages 130-179). Answer the following five questions that relate to these five studies. Integrate the material from your textbook, class lectures, class presentations, class discussions, and additional readings.

11. In reference to Study A, what operational definitions did the researchers employ for the terms "financial abuse" and "financial exploitation?" What other operational definitions could the study have included to make the findings more useful to the reader?

12. How did the researcher in Study B demonstrate the reliability of the measurement while using content analysis?

13. What level of data is reflected in each of the seven tables in the report of Study C? Justify your response.

14. In Study D, what obstacles to reliability *and* validity did the researchers probably encounter in attempting to measure the variable "frequency of sexual activity" among respondents who had suffered spinal cord injuries?

15. Why is the validity of the measurement of clients' evaluation of their caseworkers in Study E questionable? Would you expect their evaluations to be reliable? Explain.

Name:_____

Unit 14
Data Collection Instruments

Research studies that focus on the answering of research questions or the testing of hypotheses often rely heavily upon the use of standardized data collection instruments. Many types of data collection instruments are available through journals and publishing houses.

Anastas, J.W. & MacDonald, M.L. (1994). *Research design for social work and the human services.* New York: Lexington. **315-407**

Babbie, E.R. (1995). *The practice of social research* (7th ed.). Belmont, CA: Wadsworth. **139-182**

Bailey, K.D. (1994). *Methods of social research* (4th ed.). New York: Free Press. **106-146, 350-375**

DePoy, E. & Gitlin, L.N. (1994). *Introduction to research.* St. Louis, MO: Mosby. **199-202, 210-211, 225-227**

Frankfort-Nachmias, C. & Nachmias, D. (1992). *Research methods in the social sciences* (4th ed.). New York: St. Martin's Press. **239-269**

Grinnell, R.M., Jr. (Ed.) (1993). *Social work research and evaluation* (4th ed.). Itasca, IL: F.E. Peacock. **198-241**

Judd, C.M., Smith E.R., & Kidder, L.H. (1991). *Research methods in social relations* (6th ed.). Fort Worth, TX: Harcourt Brace Jovanovich. **145-170, 228-253**

Leedy, P.D. (1993). *Practical research* (5th ed.). New York: Macmillan. **187-199**

Marlow, C. (1993). *Research methods for generalist social work.* Pacific Grove, CA: Brooks/Cole. **75, 83-87**

Monette, D.R., Sullivan, T.J., & DeJong, C.R. (1994). *Applied social research* (3rd ed.). Fort Worth, TX: Harcourt Brace. **153-172, 340-363**

Neuman, W.L. (1994). *Social research methods* (2nd ed.). Boston, MA: Allyn & Bacon. **145-168, 232-234**

Royse, D.D. (1995). *Research methods in social work* (2nd ed.). Chicago, IL: Nelson-Hall. **33-36, 105-141**

Rubin, A. & Babbie, E. (1993). *Research methods for social work* (2nd ed.). Pacific Grove, CA: Brooks/Cole. **182-216**

Singleton, R.A., Jr., Straits, B.C., & Miller Straits, M. (1993). *Approaches to social research* (2nd ed.). New York: Oxford. **282-310, 391-402**

Williams, M., Tutty, L.M., & Grinnell, R.M., Jr. (1995). *Research in social work* (2nd ed.). Itasca, IL: F.E. Peacock. **115-132, 277-282**

Yegidis, B.L. & Weinbach, R.W. (1996). *Research methods for social workers* (2nd ed). Boston, MA: Allyn & Bacon. **179-193**

STUDY QUESTIONS: Answer the following ten questions in the space provided below each question. Use material from your textbook, class lectures, class presentations, class discussions, and other additional readings as necessary.

1. Explain why the sequencing of items in a data collection instrument is important and how a lack of attention to it may bias the data collected. Provide an example.

2. What is an open-ended questionnaire item? Provide an original example. When should such an item be used?

3. What is a closed-ended (fixed-alternative) item? Provide an original example. When should such an item be used?

4. Why is it sometimes necessary to use an index or scale to measure a variable rather than an open-ended or closed-ended question? Provide an example of such a situation.

5. In the first stages of scale construction, items are included because they appear to have "face validity." What does this mean?

6. Describe two different ways that you might validate a newly constructed scale designed to measure "attitudes toward abortion."

7. How is the purpose of an attitude scale different from a test of knowledge? Give an example of an item from each that illustrates the difference.

8. List three errors to avoid in the wording of attitude statements. Give an example of each.

9. Name a type of scaling technique that employs the use of "judges" and describe how this technique can be used.

10. What does it mean when we say that items are "weighted" within a given scale?

APPLICATION QUESTIONS: Refer to Research Studies A, C, D, and E (pages 130-140, 149-179). Answer the following five questions that relate to these four studies. Integrate the material from your textbook, class lectures, class presentations, class discussions, and additional readings.

11. Why do you think the researchers in Study A used a structured schedule to collect their data? What function did it perform when conducting a secondary data analysis?

12. Why were open-ended questions more appropriate for data collection in Study C than closed-ended questions?

13. Could the fact that some data in Study D were collected using in-person interviews and most were collected using telephone interviews been problematic in any way? Explain.

14. What problems do you think the researchers in Study E might have encountered in using Likert-scaled mailed questionnaires to obtain data from public welfare clients?

15. In reference to Study E, what method was used to pilot test the questionnaires used? What would have been a better way to pilot test this data collection instrument?

Unit 15
Univariate Data Analysis

When vast amounts of data are collected it is often desirable to sort and display them in summary form. This technique is often known as data reduction and employs tables, graphs, and various other descriptive techniques to summarize the data.

Anastas, J.W. & MacDonald, M.L. (1994). *Research design for social work and the human services*. New York: Lexington. **411-467**

Babbie, E.R. (1995). *The practice of social research* (7th ed.). Belmont, CA: Wadsworth. **376-384**

Bailey, K.D. (1994). *Methods of social research* (4th ed.). New York: Free Press. **337-345, 378-389**

DePoy, E. & Gitlin, L.N. (1994). *Introduction to research*. St. Louis, MO: Mosby. **229-236, 237-252**

Frankfort-Nachmias, C. & Nachmias, D. (1992). *Research methods in the social sciences* (4th ed.). New York: St. Martin's Press. **339-367**

Grinnell, R.M., Jr. (Ed.) (1993). *Social work research and evaluation* (4th ed.). Itasca, IL: F.E. Peacock. **not covered**

Judd, C.M., Smith E.R., & Kidder, L.H. (1991). *Research methods in social relations* (6th ed.). Fort Worth, TX: Harcourt Brace Jovanovich. **351-372**

Leedy, P.D. (1993). *Practical research* (5th ed.). New York: Macmillan. **42-45, 243-273**

Marlow, C. (1993). *Research methods for generalist social work*. Pacific Grove, CA: Brooks/Cole. **189-210**

Monette, D.R., Sullivan, T.J., & DeJong, C.R. (1994). *Applied social research* (3rd ed.). Fort Worth, TX: Harcourt Brace. **364-373**

Neuman, W.L. (1994). *Social research methods* (2nd ed.). Boston, MA: Allyn & Bacon. **282-294**

Royse, D.D. (1995). *Research methods in social work* (2nd ed.). Chicago, IL: Nelson-Hall. **239-244**

Rubin, A. & Babbie, E. (1993). *Research methods for social work* (2nd ed.). Pacific Grove, CA: Brooks/Cole. **449-475**

Singleton, R.A., Jr., Straits, B.C., & Miller Straits, M. (1993). *Approaches to social research* (2nd ed.). New York: Oxford. **425-434**

Williams, M., Tutty, L.M., & Grinnell, R.M., Jr. (1995). *Research in social work* (2nd ed.). Itasca, IL: F.E. Peacock. **283-293**

Yegidis, B.L. & Weinbach, R.W. (1996). *Research methods for social workers* (2nd ed). Boston, MA: Allyn & Bacon. **195-203**

STUDY QUESTIONS: Answer the following ten questions in the space provided below each question. Use material from your textbook, class lectures, class presentations, class discussions, and other additional readings as necessary.

1. Name three types of information about the distribution of a variable that can be displayed in a frequency distribution table.

2. Draw and label below two different graphs that can be used to display nominal level data.

3. Draw and label below two different graphs that can be used to display interval or ratio level data.

4. What do the mode, median, and mean tell us about the distribution of a variable? How do they differ?

5. What does a measure of dispersion (variability) tell us about the distribution of a variable?

6. What is the difference between the range and the interquartile range? When should the latter be used to describe the dispersion of a variable?

7. What does it mean when we say that a variable is normally distributed? Draw a picture of a normal curve distribution below, indicating where the mode, median, and mean would fall.

8. What is a positively-skewed distribution? Draw one below.

9. Add the standard deviation indicators to the normal curve that you drew in your answer to Question 7. In a normal distribution, approximately what percent of all case values fall within one standard deviation from the mean?

10. What are standard scores (z-scores) and how can they be used to understand the scores of individual clients on standardized tests?

APPLICATION QUESTIONS: Refer to Research Studies A, B, C, D, and E (pages 130-179). Answer the following five questions that relate to these five studies. Integrate the material from your textbook, class lectures, class presentations, class discussions, and additional readings.

11. In reference to Study A, what measures of descriptive statistics did the researchers use? Would the addition of a measure of central tendency to the tables in the report been helpful to the reader? Why or why not?

12. In reference to Study B, what would the addition of a cumulative frequency column to Table B.1 tell the reader? What would the numbers in it be (list them from top to bottom)?

13. In reference to Study C, how might the use of graphs have been helpful to the reader in visualizing the study's findings? Provide examples.

14. In reference to Study D, what would the addition of standard deviations or ranges to Tables D.2 and D.3 tell us about the scores of persons who have suffered spinal cord injuries on the scales used? Why is their absence a problem for the reader?

15. In reference to Study E, was the age of the eligibility workers who were research participants normally distributed, positively skewed, or negatively skewed? Justify your answer.

Name:_____

Unit 16
Inferential Data Analysis

Usually, a researcher hopes to learn something about a population by studying a research sample. Inferential data analyses help determine if the findings of a research study obtained from a research sample are generalizable to the population from which the sample was drawn.

Anastas, J.W. & MacDonald, M.L. (1994). *Research design for social work and the human services.* New York: Lexington. **468-508**

Babbie, E.R. (1995). *The practice of social research* (7th ed.). Belmont, CA: Wadsworth. **430-440**

Bailey, K.D. (1994). *Methods of social research* (4th ed.). New York: Free Press. **389-410**

DePoy, E. & Gitlin, L.N. (1994). *Introduction to research.* St. Louis, MO: Mosby. **252-262**

Frankfort-Nachmias, C. & Nachmias, D. (1992). *Research methods in the social sciences* (4th ed.). New York: St. Martin's Press. **369-425**

Grinnell, R.M., Jr. (Ed.) (1993). *Social work research and evaluation* (4th ed.). Itasca, IL: F.E. Peacock. **not covered**

Judd, C.M., Smith E.R., & Kidder, L.H. (1991). *Research methods in social relations* (6th ed.). Fort Worth, TX: Harcourt Brace Jovanovich. **373-424**

Leedy, P.D. (1993). *Practical research* (5th ed.). New York: Macmillan. **278-294**

Marlow, C. (1993). *Research methods for generalist social work.* Pacific Grove, CA: Brooks/Cole. **213-229**

Monette, D.R., Sullivan, T.J., & DeJong, C.R. (1994). *Applied social research* (3rd ed.). Fort Worth, TX: Harcourt Brace. **373-394**

Neuman, W.L. (1994). *Social research methods* (2nd ed.). Boston, MA: Allyn & Bacon. **294-313**

Royse, D.D. (1995). *Research methods in social work* (2nd ed.). Chicago, IL: Nelson-Hall. **244-255**

Rubin, A. & Babbie, E. (1993). *Research methods for social work* (2nd ed.). Pacific Grove, CA: Brooks/Cole. **476-533**

Singleton, R.A., Jr., Straits, B.C., & Miller Straits, M. (1993). *Approaches to social research* (2nd ed.). New York: Oxford. **434-470**

Williams, M., Tutty, L.M., & Grinnell, R.M., Jr. (1995). *Research in social work* (2nd ed.). Itasca, IL: F.E. Peacock. **293-303**

Yegidis, B.L. & Weinbach, R.W. (1996). *Research methods for social workers* (2nd ed). Boston, MA: Allyn & Bacon. **200-201**

STUDY QUESTIONS: Answer the following ten questions in the space provided below each question. Use material from your textbook, class lectures, class presentations, class discussions, and other additional readings as necessary.

1. What are rival hypotheses? What are some of the rival hypotheses that might explain an apparent relationship between "type of treatment (A or B)" and "treatment success" within a sample of clients who abuse alcohol?

2. Until a statistical analysis is performed, a skeptic might say that the apparent relationship may be attributable to chance. What does that mean?

3. If, using statistical testing, we were able to demonstrate that the relationship between two variables was "statistically significant at the .05 level" what would that mean?

4. In relation to Question 3, does a statistically significant finding mean a substantive one? Why or why not?

5. What is the difference between a one-tailed (directional) hypothesis and a two-tailed (non-directional) hypothesis? Provide an example of each using the two variables in Question 1.

6. What is the "null" form of a research hypothesis? State the hypotheses in your answer to Question 5 in their null form.

7. When, in testing a one-tailed or two-tailed hypothesis, a researcher concludes that it is possible to "reject the null hypothesis" what does that mean?

8. What are Type I and Type II errors? Provide a social work example of each one.

9. When we say that one statistical test of significance is more powerful than another one, what does that mean? What the main factors affect the statistical power of a test?

10. What is the difference between a bivariate test of significance and a multivariate one?

APPLICATION QUESTIONS: Refer to Research Studies A, B, C, and D (pages 130-170). Answer the following five questions that relate to these four studies. Integrate the material from your textbook, class lectures, class presentations, class discussions, and additional readings.

11. Do you think that the researchers in Study A were justified in concluding that older persons with certain demographic characteristics are at risk for financial abuse? Why or why not?

12. Does the data analysis in the report of Study B suggest that the change in documentation in policy statements after 1983 probably reflects a real change in behavior or is that it may be the work of chance? Explain your answer.

13. Why would you not expect that Study C would have employed hypothesis testing and inferential statistics to answer the research question?

14. In reference to Study D, what statistical test could have been used to further examine the data in Table D.1? State the null form of a hypothesis relating the variables "gender" and "lack of opportunity."

15. The report of Study D notes that "clients in urban counties were more likely to state that their workers did not spend enough time with them than clients in rural areas." Why is the finding that the two variables reflect a statistically significant relationship not surprising, and probably not substantive? Explain.

Part II
Sample Research Studies

Research Study A

VICTIMIZATION OF THE ELDERLY:
INDIVIDUAL AND FAMILY CHARACTERISTICS
OF FINANCIAL ABUSE

Jeffery A. Giordano, Bonnie L. Yegidis, and Nan Hervig Giordano

Older people are particularly vulnerable to financial abuse. This study isolated financial abuse from other forms of abuse. Data from two hundred and forty-six subjects were analyzed to produce descriptive profiles of the abused and the perpetrator. A sub-group of severely financially abused elderly was also examined. The profile of the typical financially abused victim was a white female widow over 75 years old with a physical illness. Financially abused elderly were found to be victimized primarily by friends and relatives. The findings on perpetrators suggest that social workers can detect abuse from social indicators such as unemployment, impairments and relationships problems, and that treatment should be directed toward reducing the stress of care giving.

VICTIMIZATION OF THE ELDERLY takes many forms. The elderly, like any other segment of the population, are vulnerable to criminal acts such as robbery, burglary, auto theft, aggravated assault, purse snatching or pick-pocketing. Financial exploitation in the form of bunko games or fraud produces a disproportionate number of victims among the elderly. Further criminal abuse of the elderly is often perpetrated by intimates, such as friends, relatives and human service practitioners. This type of victimization is typically dealt with by social workers in the human service system rather than by police. While the literature on elder abuse has become quite extensive, limited information exists on financial abuse victims.

There are six identified types of elder abuse: physical abuse, negligence, financial exploitation, psychological abuse, violation of rights and self-neglect (Giordano & Giordano, 1984). Physical abuse and negligence have received the most attention in the literature even though financial abuse has been documented to be quite extensive. Legal Research Services for the Elderly (1979) estimated that 31% of the elderly population are victims of financial abuse. In a study of elder abuse conducted in Texas, financial abuse was the most frequent type of abuse recorded (Anderson, 1984).

The focus of this research is on financial abuse of the elderly. Financial abuse is a form of financial exploitation that involves wrongful acquisitions of money or valuable objects belonging to an elderly person by friends, relatives or caretakers.

Financial exploitation, a much broader category, involves theft or wrongful acquisition of money or objects of value by force or misrepresentation. Activities that exploit the elderly have become so common that certain schemes such as "bait-and-switch" and the "bank examiner" are well-known to the public and authorities. Consumer fraud is an area where the elderly are disproportionately represented as victims (Malinchak & Wright, 1978, 1981). Health frauds such as miracle cures, glorified potions and medical quackery are a growing area of exploitation of the elderly who are concerned with their health and bodies (Geis, 1976). In our society, the perpetrator of financial exploitation is viewed as a criminal.

No clear-cut consensus of criminal attribution exists for financial abuse of the elderly if or when the perpetrator is an acquaintance, often a family member and frequently a person in need of help. While financial abuse does represent a violation of law, the law breaker, in this instance, is an individual who typically has not adopted a life style of criminal behavior or criminal deception. Further, the problem of elder abuse cannot be understood from a single act of victimization with questionable motives, but rather from patterns of relationships between individuals known to one another where the elderly person is exploited (Giordano & Giordano, 1984; Yin, 1986).

Older persons are particularly vulnerable to financial abuse. The presence of chronic illness, isolation and dependency experienced by some elderly increase their vulnerability (McGhee, 1983). Certainly the high incidence of widowhood in which elderly individuals either live alone or with someone in a dependent circumstance provides opportunity for financial abuse. Some of the fears that aging people experience, such as a fear of death or loss of independence, may lead to greater vulnerability for financial abuse.

Current theories of abuse are more applicable to physical abuse, neglect and psychological abuse than to financial abuse (Yin, 1986). An explanatory theory of financial abuse would have to include concepts of family relationships, interpersonal relationships, and dependency relationships. Studies to date have documented that most financial abuse is perpetrated by family members (Lau & Kosberg, 1978; Block & Sinnott, 1979). However, these studies were based on small samples or secondary interviews with professionals.

The study reported in this article draws data from a large sample of abused elderly that appear in case records of abuse (Giordano, 1982). This study seeks to expand the knowledge specific to financial abuse on which to base assessment and intervention. It examines the characteristics of financially abused elderly and the characteristics of their perpetrators.

METHODOLOGY

DATA ON ABUSED ELDERLY PERSONS were obtained by examining the actual case files documentation reported by victims to caseworkers investigating abuse. The caseworkers were employed by Adult Service Units of Florida's Health and Rehabilitation Services in five Florida counties. The data were from abuse cases investigated in 1982. This extensive review produced information on 600 cases of abused elderly that was transferred by the researchers to a structured schedule. An interrater reliability check conducted by two researchers was completed and agreement was reached on 95% of the cases. Subjects were selected if the person was 60 years of age or older, there was a documented objectional acquisition of valuables, and the subject was not in a nursing home or institution. Three categories of data were obtained: (1) type of abuse, (2) individual characteristics of the victim and of the perpetrator, and (3) family circumstances for both the victim and the perpetrator.

An extensive literature search was conducted to identify relevant variables likely to be associated with elder abuse. Table A.1 presents all 33 variables used in the analysis of the financially abused, (Block & Sinnott, 1979; Giordano, 1982; O'Rourke, 1981; Pedrick-Comell & Gelles, 1981). The number of financially abused elders was 246, and the number of severely abused, which will be described as a subgroup, was 98. The group of 246 financially abused are the subjects for this study. A frequency distribution with measures of central tendency and dispersion was used to describe the financially abused elder, the family situation, and the perpetrator. Those variables in which a group could be considered homogenous were used to develop profiles of the abuse victims and the perpetrators.

FINDINGS

A LARGE NUMBER OF VARIABLES thought to be associated with or descriptive of abuse victims and perpetrators was examined. A description of the entire group of financially abused elders (abused and severely abused) and their perpetrators as well as a description of the subgroup of severely financially abused elders and their perpetrators is presented in the following section.

The Financially Abused

An overwhelming majority of the financially abused in this study were white females living with a relative other than their spouses. These victims ranged in age from 60-98 with a mean age of 77 ($SD = 9.2$) and a modal age of 80. Two-thirds of the victims were living with the perpetrator at the time of the abuse. Fully 83% of the victims were widowed and almost 90% had income levels below $14,000 a year.

Of the victims who were married (13%), some level of marital dysfunctioning was present in more than 25% of the cases. Almost half of the financially abused clients were assessed as having problems in either psychological or intellectual functioning and nearly 90% were reported as being physically ill. Only slightly more than one-quarter of the clients actually had a physical handicap. While there was almost no evidence of alcohol use by the victims, nearly 60% of them were taking prescription medications during the period of the abuse. Physical abuse, in addition to financial abuse, was present in 28% of the cases and more than one-third of the clients were suffering from neglect. There was evidence of psychological abuse in one-quarter of the cases.

TABLE A.1
IDENTIFIED ELDER ABUSE VARIABLES

Victim	Perpetrator	Other Variables
1. Age	1. Age	1. With whom the victim lives
2. Gender	2. Gender	2. Number of abuse incidents
3. Race	3. Race	3. Relationship of perpetrator
4. Marital status	4. Marital status	4. Number of persons in the home
5. Marital problems	5. Alcohol use	5. Number of children in the home
6. Alcohol use	6. Drug use	6. Elder parent-adult child conflicts
7. Drug use	7. Psychological	7. Adult child-sibling conflicts
8. Psychological problems	8. Physical handicaps	8. Living with perpetrator
9. Physical handicaps	9. Physical illness	
10. Physical illness	10. Financial problems	
11. Intellectual impairments	11. Employment	
12. Income	12. Income	
	13. Marital problems	

TABLE A.2

DESCRIPTION OF THE FINANCIALLY ABUSED

	N	%
Gender:		
Male	71	29.0
Female	175	71.0
Race:		
White	200	81.3
Black	33	13.4
Hispanic	13	5.3
Income Level:		
Below $7,000	177	72.0
$7,000–$14,000	41	16.7
$14,000–$30,000	21	8.5
Over $30,000	7	2.8
Marital Status:		
Married	31	13.0
Divorced/Separated	7	2.8
Widowed	204	83.0
Never Married	3	1.0

The Perpetrators

Perpetrators ranged in age from 13-90 with a mean age of 47.7 ($SD = 14.3$) and a modal age of 38. Nearly half were married and fully 95% had annual incomes below $14,000 a year. At the time of the abuse, more than half were unemployed. Perpetrators were found to be related to their victims in 68% of the cases. However, a large percentage (32%) were nonrelatives. Small percentages of the perpetrators were reported to have psychological problems (15%), financial difficulties (17%), or marital problems (9.4%). There was evidence of elderly parent-child conflicts in 17% of the cases. In addition, slightly more than one-quarter of the perpetrators were found to be using alcohol during the period of abuse. Only 7.5% were reported to be taking medication.

In only 21 of the 246 cases was there record of a second perpetrator. In most cases, the second perpetrator was the victim's daughter-in-law. Since the only variable that emerged as being worthy of note was the relationship of the second perpetrator to the victim, further analyses of second perpetrator characteristics will not be presented.

The Severely Financially Abused

Of the 246 abuse cases, 98 individuals were categorized as being severely financially abused according to the previously defined criterion. Both the severely financially abused victims and their perpetrators are described in Table A.4. More than half of the severely abused clients were living with the perpetrator at the time of the abuse. A substantial majority of the severely

TABLE A.3
DESCRIPTION OF THE PERPETRATORS ($N = 246$)

	N	$\%$
Gender:		
Male	128	52.0
Female	116	48.0
Race:		
White	207	84.1
Black	26	10.6
Hispanic	13	5.3
Income Level:		
Below $7,000	121	50.4
$7,000–$14,000	84	35.0
$14,000–$30,000	32	13.3
Over $30,000	3	1.2
Marital Status:		
Married	120	48.8
Divorced/Separated	78	32.1
Widowed	15	6.1
Never Married	32	13.0
Relationship to Victim:		
Son/daughter/son-in-law	87	35.4
Spouse	18	7.3
Grandchild	24	9.8
Sister	4	1.6
Other relative	33	13.4
	166	67.5
Non-relative:	79	32.1

financially abused (65%) were having difficulties that required the use of prescription drugs. Additionally, these individuals were found to have some difficulty in psychological functioning (57%), physical functioning (91%), or intellectual functioning (58%).

These findings suggest that clients who suffer from physical, psychological or intellectual impairments are at greater risk of being financially abused than those who are not similarly impaired. Only small percentages of the severely financially abused also showed evidence of physical abuse (16%) or psychological abuse (15%). However, nearly one-third of these clients suffered from neglect.

Perpetrators of the Severely Abused

Fully three-fourths of the perpetrators were relatives of the victims, while only one-fourth were non-relatives. The perpetrator-relative was most likely to be a married son. Other family perpetrators were grandchildren, daughters, spouses or siblings. The perpetrators ranged in age from 14 to 83 with a mean age of 47.6 ($SD = 14.5$) and a modal age of 60. At the time of the abuse, the perpetrator was

TABLE A.4
DESCRIPTION OF THE SEVERELY
FINANCIALLY ABUSED (*N* = 98)

	N	*%*
Gender:		
Male	31	31.6
Female	67	68.4
Race:		
White	85	86.7
Black	11	11.2
Hispanic	2	2.0
Income Level:		
Below $7,000	61	62.2
$7,000–$14,000	15	15.3
$14,000–$30,000	16	16.3
Over $30,000	6	6.2
Marital Status:		
Married	15	15.3
Divorced/Separated	4	4.1
Widowed	78	79.6
Never Married	1	1.0

most likely to be unemployed.

The perpetrators showed almost no evidence of physical illness. However, nearly 20% were having financial problems, 15% were having marital difficulties, and 11% were suffering from psychological dysfunctioning. As might be expected, almost 20% of the cases showed evidence of elder parent-adult conflict. There was also evidence that perpetrators were using alcohol (20%) during the period of abuse.

DISCUSSION

PROFILES OF THE VICTIMS and perpetrators will be presented and a subgroup of the severely financially abused will be distinguished from the larger group. Distinct profiles of the abused and the abuser have been attempted in many studies with little consistency (Pillemer & Wolf, 1981). However, profiles across types of abuse assume similarities which have been shown to be minimal (Giordano, 1982). The following profiles are based on the 246 financially abused individuals and the perpetrators examined in this study.

Victim Profile

A clear profile of the typical victim of financial abuse reveals a person who is a white, elderly, female widow over 75 years of age, with a physical illness, and impairment in either the psychological, intellectual or physical domain. The victim is likely to be taking prescription drugs to treat an illness. Additionally, she may also be suffering from neglect, psychological abuse or physical abuse.

TABLE A.5
DESCRIPTION OF PERPETRATORS OF THE
SEVERELY FINANCIALLY ABUSED ($N = 98$)

	N	%
Gender:		
Male	56	57.1
Female	42	42.9
Race:		
White	87	88.3
Black	9	9.2
Hispanic	2	2.0
Income Level:		
Below $7,000	39	40.6
$7,000–$14,000	37	38.5
$14,000–$30,000	18	18.2
Over $30,000	2	2.1
Marital Status:		
Married	48	49.0
Divorced/Separated	35	35.7
Widowed	4	4.1
Never Married	11	11.2
Relationship to Victim:		
Son/daughter/son-in-law	32	31.6
Spouse	7	7.1
Grandchild	11	11.2
Other relative	<u>14</u>	<u>14.3</u>
	64	64.2
Non-relative:	34	34.7

A comparison of the severely abused cases ($n = 98$) to the group of victims as a whole ($n = 246$) reveals marked similarities on almost every demographic variable of the study. The distribution of race, age, gender and marital status were nearly identical for the two groups. The percentages of physical illness for the two groups were also identical. However, the severely financially abused had more than twice as many subjects with incomes above $14,000 per year. Additionally, this group showed slightly greater impairment in the psychological and intellectual domains and were more likely to be taking prescription medication.

The severely financially abused respondents showed less physical abuse and less psychological abuse than the larger group of financially abused cases, although rates for neglect were identical. Finally, the severely financially abused victims were somewhat less likely to be living with the perpetrator at the time of the abuse.

The profile shows that victims of financial abuse are older women. These women are vulnerable to financial abuse for a number of interrelated reasons. First of all, they tend to outlive their husbands. This means that when their health fails, they are likely to be confronted with the decision of whether to reside in a care facility or with a family member. For most people, the fear of residing and possibly dying in a nursing home is strong. Thus the preferred choice is to make one's home with a family member, who is often the adult child. Even if their treatment is abusive, it may seem preferable to, being "put away."

Additionally, elderly women may have had minimal experience in management of financial resources. This lack of knowledge and experience makes them vulnerable to financial exploitation. Family care givers are the logical persons to manage an elderly person's banking, insurance policies and so forth. For a person who has limited experience with finances this assistance may even be welcome.

Many abused women are taking prescription medication which can influence their ability to manage their own affairs, financial or otherwise. Consequently, for these reasons, elderly women residing with family care givers are particularly vulnerable to financial abuse. This phenomenon is consistent with the findings of other researchers who have studied elder abuse (Kosberg, 1983).

Perpetrator Profile

A profile of the perpetrators suggests that these individuals are males or females of similar race to the victims. They are likely to be the married, adult children of the victims. The perpetrators are usually unemployed with income levels at or below the poverty level.

A comparison of the perpetrators for the two groups (abused and severely abused) also reveals similarities in demographic characteristics. However, the perpetrators of the severely abused were slightly more likely to be male than female. The perpetrators of the severely abused had somewhat greater annual incomes than the perpetrators of the large group. Both groups of perpetrators were equally likely to be unemployed. The only characteristic that emerged as being truly distinct between the two groups of perpetrators was the modal age of the severely abusive perpetrator, which was 60. For the financially abused group as a whole, the age of the perpetrator was 38. This age difference and information on the relationship to the victims suggests that perpetrators of the severely abused are much more likely to be elderly children or the spouse of the victims.

LIMITATIONS AND FUTURE RESEARCH

THE SUBJECTS OF THIS STUDY were drawn from case files of those who were previously determined as having been abused, to develop profiles of abused elders and their perpetrators. While this provides valuable information on the characteristics of this population, generalization to larger populations is limited. The characteristics that emerged may be helpful in determining potential for abuse but there may be other variables and circumstances that would emerge from a different or broader population. Additional research that expands the search for variables is needed. Further, other data gathering methods such as structured interviews of the abused and abuser could be employed to overcome the limitations of existing information from case files.

IMPLICATIONS AND INTERVENTIONS

IT HAS FREQUENTLY BEEN SAID that financial abuse can be difficult to detect, investigate and prove (Quinn & Tomita, 1986). This is so because there has not been a research knowledge base from which to predict and detect financial abuse. Practice wisdom has dominated, particularly in protective services, where the primary mode has been investigative rather than evaluative. Indeed, recommended procedures and lists of indicators that would lead to the detection of financial abuse include such things as the investigation of bank accounts, observation of the lack of luxuries in the home, inquiry as to the absence of certain personal items, and review of documents to check the signature of the elderly person.

A more desirable approach in examining abuse situations is the use of the focused interview with the elderly person and the caretaker. Such an interview could incorporate a variety of questions and observations that would bring the worker to the conclusion that abuse is likely to occur or is probably occurring. Such questions and observations could be grounded in the profile information of financial abuse victims and the perpetrators. For example, when working with an elderly widow with a physical illness, where the caretaker is unemployed and experiencing conflicts with another member of the family, one would begin to suspect that the elderly widow is "at risk" of being financially abused.

Adult protective services, which is designed to help abused older people, is the primary program that addresses elder abuse. However, by the time that an abused elderly person begins to receive these services, the abuse has often been long standing, and corrective action and intervention are difficult. Large numbers of service professionals who have contact with the elderly through a variety of other services, particularly health services, are in a better position for early detection of financial abuse. Unfortunately, existing systematic assessment and evaluative techniques list variables associated with abuse that have not been documented (Tomital 1982).

Previous research has shown that the severity of the abuse has very little relation to the type of intervention chosen or initiated by service providers (Phillips & Rempushecki, 1986). Some researchers would determine severity by monetary value or the frequency of abuse, but that has minimal value when interventions are the consideration. This study determined severity by the level of regard for the victim; providing important information for the practitioner. It was found that severe financial abuse frequently involves another older adult, which indicates that it is either a spouse or an adult child also struggling with the normal problems of aging. Special attention needs to be paid to this point since it has been suggested that many protective service workers may be sympathetic to older adults struggling with the problems of aging and thereby exercise restraint with regard to appropriate interventions.

It was found in this study and previous studies, that the financial abuser is a care giver, not a criminal who is abnormal or disturbed. Therefore, assessment should be situational, including family members and when appropriate, non-relative care givers. The focus of such an assessment must have a dual purpose: first, to confirm the suspected financial abuse, and second, to determine the characteristics that will lead to the appropriate intervention for the given situation.

When considering intervention methods it appears that intervention with the care giver is equally, if not more, important than direct intervention with the victim. While the victim needs protection, the care giver needs the support and treatment. Care givers who receive the least support from human services and friends often express the feelings of frustration and discontent.

In this research, relationship variables such as marital problems or adult-parent conflict did not emerge as dominant characteristics on which to focus intervention. What did emerge is that care givers need support in the way of relief such as respite care, education, employment, and financial assistance. Further, direct assistance with care giving, as well as participation in support groups with other care givers, seems to be the more appropriate types of interventions indicated by these findings.

Preventive intervention would be of benefit to both the potential victim and the care giver. Educational programs such as preretirement and post retirement seminars might be useful interventions. These programs provide information and resources for dealing with both financial matters and interpersonal relationships (Giordano & Giordano, 1983). Private case management services for the elderly have emerged as an option to assist care givers who can afford them.

These services offered by social workers and gerontologists provide assistance on a fee-for-service basis. Services such as maintaining financial records, routine health checks, advice on investments, and assistance in obtaining services from the human and health service system are offered. Contracted case management services remove some of the burden from family care givers and thereby reduce frustration and stress. Private case management services often are free from the bureaucratic and potential restraints that frequently operate to limit protective service availability to care givers. While no research has been conducted on private case management services for the elderly, this is an emerging area of service which may help to prevent financial abuse.

REFERENCES

Anderson, J. (1984). A *survey of abuse of the elderly in Texas.* Paper presented at the 27th Annual Scientific Meeting of the Gerontological Society, San Antonio, Texas (ERIC Document Reproduction Service No. 25487).

Block, M. & Sinnott, J.D. (Eds.). (1979). *The battered elder syndrome: An exploratory study.* Unpublished manuscript, University of Maryland, Center on Aging.

Geis, G. (1976). Defrauding the elderly. In J. Goldsmith & S. Goldsmith (Eds.), *Crime and the elderly* (pp. 7-18.) Lexington, MA: D.C. Heath.

Giordano, N.H. (1982). *Individual antifamily correlates of elder abuse.* Unpublished dissertation, University of Georgia, Athens.

Giordano, N.H. & Giordano, J.A. (1984). Elder abuse: A review of the literature. *Social Work, 29,* 232-236.

Giordano, H.N. & Giordano, J.A. (1983). A classification of preretirement programs: In search of new model, *Educational Gerontology 9,* 123-137.

Kosberg, J. (1983). *Abuse and maltreatment of the elderly: Causes and interventions.* Boston: John Wright.

Lau, E. & Kosberg, J. (1978). *Abuse of the elderly by informal care providers: Practice and research issues.* Paper presented at the 31st Annual Meeting of the Gerontological Society, Dallas, TX.

Legal Research Services for the Elderly, (1979). Elder abuse in Massachusetts: A survey of professionals and paraprofessionals. Unpublished manuscript.

Malinchak, A.A. & Wright, D. (1978). Older Americans and crime: The scope of elderly victimization. *Aging, 28,* 10-16.

Malinchak, A.A. & Wright, D. (1981). *Older Americans and crime: The scope of elderly victimization.* U.S. House of Representatives Sub-Committee on Aging. U.S. Printing Office.

McGhee, J.L. (I 983). The vulnerability of elderly consumers. *Intervention Journal of Aging and Human Development, 17,* 223-241.

O'Rourke, M. (1981). *Elder abuse: The state of the art.* Paper presented at the National Conference on the Abuse of Older Persons, Boston, MA.

Pedrick-Comell, C. & Gelles, R.J. (1981). *Elder abuse: The status of current knowledge.* Paper presented at the National Conference on Abuse of Older Persons, Boston, MA.

Phillips, L.R. & Rempushecki, V.F. (1986). Making decisions about the elder abuse. *Social Casework, 67,* 131-140.

Pillemer, K. & Wolf, R.S. (Eds.). (1981). *Elder abuse: Conflict in the family.* Dover, MA: Aubom House.

Quinn, M.J. & Tomita, S.K. (1986). *Elder abuse and neglect, causes, diagnosis, and intervention strategies.* New York: Springer.

Tomita, S.K. (1982). Detection and treatment of elderly abuse and neglect: A protocol for health care professionals. *PT and OT in Geriatrics 2,* 27-51.

Yin, P. (1986) *Victimization and the aged.* Springfield, IL: Charles C. Thomas.

Research Study B

DOES THE SOCIAL WORK PROFESSION VALUE RESEARCH BASED KNOWLEDGE AS A BASIS FOR SOCIAL POLICY?

Beth Spenciner Rosenthal

A content analysis of NASW's policy statements was undertaken to determine the degree to which verified knowledge informs social work's public policy stance. The data reveal that the overall documentation of knowledge is low and that there is little advocation of specific research needed to address knowledge gaps. The profession likely would be more influential in the policy arena if it better documented its knowledge beliefs in addition to promulgating its value positions.

TENSION REGARDING THE APPROPRIATE role of knowledge, as distinguished from values, as a basis for social work practice has occupied a prominent place in the professional literature for over 30 years (Bartlett, 1958, 1970; Gordon, 1962; Greenwood, 1957; Karger, 1983; Lewis, 1982; Simpson, 1978; Weick, 1987; Williams & Hopps, 1987, 1988). The present paper extends this discussion by focusing explicitly on the policy positions taken by the social work profession and by differentiating the degree to which the relevant knowledge base has been validated.

Bartlett (1970) conceptually differentiated between values and knowledge: "Value statements refer to what is preferred; knowledge statements to what is confirmed or confirmable" (p. 63). Values refer to what is good and desirable; they are subjective judgments and not empirically demonstrable. Knowledge, on the other hand, refers to a statement about experience that is potentially verifiable by relatively objective procedures. Knowledge is the body of potentially verifiable statements of relationships among events in the real world.

Knowledge and values interact in determining professional action. Knowledge statements describe what is the perceived circumstance in the real world; values produce an evaluation of that situation as desirable or undesirable. If the circumstance is less desirable than an alternative one, values impel to action to change the circumstance. Knowledge statements, describing the relations among events in the real world, provide guidance regarding the actions that may be taken to change the present circumstance into one that is more desirable.

Note that the key to the knowledge realm, in Bartlett's conceptualization, is a statement's capability of being verified, not the condition of its already having been verified. Thus, knowledge statements may be differentiated in terms of the degree to which they have been subjected to attempts of verification and the degree to which these attempts at verification have provided confirmation. A knowledge statement may have been subjected to extensive verification attempts, the results of which confirm that it is true. But, a knowledge statement may also be widely accepted as true even though it has not yet been subjected to formal verification. Indeed, a knowledge proposition may be widely believed to be true, but turn out to be false when it is subjected to a format verification procedure.

The knowledge base of a profession is the collection of potentially verifiable statements about the phenomena of professional interest that are generally accepted by its members. These knowledge beliefs will vary in the degree to which they have already been verified and may differ in the degree to which they are valid descriptions of these phenomena. The more valid a knowledge proposition, the better guide it is to accomplishing change in the real world.

The practice knowledge base in the practice professions traditionally has been drawn primarily from the insights and accumulated experiences of the individual practitioner, and from the recorded body of collective professional experience (practice wisdom) as taught in professional schools or published in professional writing (Austin, 1991). Empirical research, the use of a set of formal relatively objective procedures that have been developed to verify knowledge propositions, has become increasingly important in the refinement of the knowledge base of most practice professions during the 20th century (Austin, 1991).

The importance to the profession of social work of the results of research has been asserted for some time (Kahn, 1954; Kirk & Fischer, 1976; National Association of Social Workers, 1964; Simpson, 1978; Weinberger & Tripodi, 1969; Williams & Hopps, 1988). Indeed, empirical research methods have been mandated as part of the curriculum for the education of professional social workers (Council on Social Work Education, 1982, 1988). Most recently a national task force has been formed "to examine the present and future role of research in the profession of social work" (Task Force on Social Work Research, 1989, p. 1).

Despite the increasing emphasis on research, content analyses of the periodical literature of the social work profession have consistently demonstrated a relatively weak research orientation on the part of the profession (Glisson, 1983, 1990; Jayaratne, 1979; Simpson, 1978; Taber & Shapiro, 1965; Weinberger & Tripodi, 1969). Austin (1991) has noted the "continuing tension between the role of professional experience and the role of research in the professional knowledge base" in social work (p. 38). Hartman (1990) has recently reasserted the legitimacy of personal experience and practice wisdom as contributors to the knowledge base of social work on a par with formal empirical research.

Thus, the knowledge beliefs that form the knowledge base for social work practice may differ in terms of the level of their validity (the degree to which they have been verified) and in terms of the basis for the claim to validity (individual experience, informal collective practice wisdom, or formal empirical research). In formal communication for the purpose of influencing beliefs and behaviors about professional practice issues, it is usual to support explicit and implicit claims for validity of knowledge assertions by presenting evidence of a confirmatory nature or citing sources of such evidence. This is especially so when claim is based on formal empirical research.

The social work profession speaks to social policy through the National Association of Social Workers (NASW) and its key policy-making body, the Delegate Assembly. Potential policy statements are submitted to the Delegate Assembly for adoption after being circulated for review and recommended changes to chapters and national units. They are further debated on the floor of the Assembly before being voted on for approval.

Over the past 20 years, the Delegate Assembly has adopted 48 different policy statements representing the profession's views regarding major social issues, such as deinstitutionalization, family policy and national health care. These policy statements have been assembled in a book, *Social Work Speaks* (National Association of Social Workers, 1988).

The statements serve three major purposes: they provide guidance both to the NASW national office and to state chapters in legislative activities by being standards against which to judge proposed legislation; they provide guidance to the NASW in legal matters by being standards against which to judge the joining in of amicus curiae (friend of the court) briefs; and they are vehicles for use in social work education because they are the articulation of the profession's ideal policies.

Thus, the social work profession's primary social policy positions are represented by its formal social policy statements as presented in *Social Work Speaks* (National Association of Social Workers, 1988). A content analysis of these statements was undertaken to describe the degree to which knowledge (as differentiated from values) infuses and informs the profession's public policy stance; and to describe the degree to which the knowledge statements reflect a reliance on formal empirical research knowledge as a source. The policy statements generally comprise two sections, a "preamble" (background and statement of issues) and "recommendations" (policy statements, per se). One would expect to find knowledge propositions describing the current state of the real world, value-based judgments of this state, and knowledge-based anticipations of the consequences of various alternative actions in the preamble section; and in the recommendations section, proposed action based on value judgments about the desirability of the outcomes of alterative actions—including the desirability of carrying out additional research to strengthen the verified knowledge base if the amount of verified knowledge was judged as being insufficient.

METHOD

THE CONTENT OF EACH POLICY STATEMENT was examined and each instance of a *knowledge statement* (i.e., potentially verifiable statement) and each instance of a *mention of need for further research* (i.e., a reference to a need to study, investigate, research or engage in other activity of formal verification of knowledge) was identified.

The knowledge statements were classified in terms of the level of documentation of empirical verification that accompanied them, using four categories: no documentation; vague documentation; informal documentation; and formal documentation.

No documentation involves bald assertions with no attempt to provide evidence of verification or source of external support. An exemplar is: "altruistic, service oriented motivation appears to be increasing for men as well as for women."

Vague documentation involves assertions accompanied by a general non-specific reference to the existence of supporting evidence such as "the literature shows," 44 social scientists assert," or "estimates indicate." An exemplar is: "Statistics indicate that poverty is multifaceted."

Informal documentation involves assertions which have no formal bibliographic citation, but do include an informal reference to a specific institutional or publication source of verification. An exemplar is: "Since the National Centers for Disease Control began its enumeration of diagnosed cases in 1981, there have been more than 44,000 persons in the United States diagnosed as having AIDS."

Formal documentation involves assertions accompanied by formal biographic citations. Each policy statement was then classified in terms of the presence or absence of a knowledge statement with each of these four levels of documentation.

The mentions of need for further research were classified in terms of the *degree of specificity* of the content of the advocated research. *Relatively specific* involves an explicit mention of the topic or issue to be studied, while *vague and general*
involves only non-specific, imprecise descriptions of the topics for study. An exemplar of a relatively specific statement is "...research ... into strategies, techniques, and innovative ways to meet the service needs of families should be supported;" and an exemplar of a vague and general statement is: "ongoing research and evaluation ... should be used..."

Each policy statement was categorized in terms of the presence or absence of each level of research topic specification. All of the above classifications were quite reliable. Reliability of the identification of *knowledge statements and mention of need for further research,* the reliability of the classifications of each instance of *knowledge statement* and a *mention of need for further research,* and the reliability of the classification of each policy statement was checked by doing the content analysis twice with the two content analyses separated by a period of two months. The results of the two content analyses were in agreement 95% of the time. Most of the disagreements arose in the area of degree of specificity of research advocated. When a disagreement between the two content analyses occurred, the content in question was examined a third time and the disagreement resolved.

FINDINGS

NEARLY ALL OF THE POLICY STATEMENTS contain some assertion of knowledge relevant to the given issue—only one of the 48 has *no* mention at all of relevant knowledge (Table B.1). All of the 47 policy statements that use knowledge contain bald assertions of knowledge with no external support. One-half contain vaguely documented knowledge assertions supported only by a general non-specific reference such as to "the literature." And approximately one-half contain knowledge assertions that are supported by some more specific documentation, either informal or formal. Many of the policy statements contain knowledge statements at two or three different levels of documentation.

The overall level of documentation of the knowledge assertions in the policy statements is rather, low, however. Approximately one-quarter contain *only* bald unsupported assertions. For another quarter of the policy statements, the highest level of documentation for a knowledge assertion is a vague non-specific reference such as to "the literature." Approximately one-quarter of them had an informal reference such as to an institutional source as the highest level of documentation. Only one-quarter of the policy statements contained a knowledge assertion with a specific bibliographic citation.

Over one-half of the policy statements contain no recommendation for additional research on the issue (Table B.2). Over one-quarter of them contain recommendations for additional research that are quite vague and general—they refer to research in general but do not specify either the nature of the research or the nature of the knowledge that is needed. Only about one-sixth of the policy

TABLE B.1

FREQUENCY WITH WHICH KNOWLEDGE ASSERTIONS
WITH VARIOUS TYPES OF SUPPORT ARE PRESENT IN POLICY STATEMENTS

Type of Support	Absolute frequency	Frequency with which this is highest level of support	Percent highest level is of total
No knowledge statement	1	1	02
Bald assertion	47	13	27
Vaguely documented	24	12	25
Informal specific documentation	12	11	23
Bibliographic citation	11	11	23

statements are relatively specific about describing the nature of the research advocated or the nature of the knowledge needed.

More recent (after 1983) policy statements were a little less likely to use bald knowledge statements and a little more likely to use an informal reference to an institutional source to support their knowledge statements (Table B.3) but this difference does not quite attain statistical significance at the .05 level. The more recent policy statements were also no more likely to recommend additional research on the issue.

DISCUSSION

THE POLICY STATEMENTS do involve knowledge assertions—only one contained no knowledge statement in its premise. But the knowledge statements tend to be so undocumented that the reader is at a loss to differentiate between well-verified facts and merely unsubstantiated assumption. Knowledge beliefs—beliefs about the relationships among events in the real world—are essential to discussion of social policy. The issue is the degree to which these beliefs need to be formally verified. The content of the policy statements indicates that the social work profession does not think that the degree of formal verification of its knowledge beliefs is an important matter.

A substantial minority of the policy statements also contain recommendations to do "research." But two-thirds of these recommendations to do research are so vague and general that they give no direction to the research, and fail even to hint at the substance of the knowledge that needs to be developed or verified.

The policy statements set the parameters for the social work profession's positions and actions on a broad range of social issues, and they are the products

TABLE B.2

FREQUENCY WITH WHICH FURTHER RESEARCH
IS ADVOCATED IN POLICY RECOMMENDATIONS

Nature of Research Recommendation	Frequency	Percent
None recommended	26	54
General recommendation, only	14	29
Specific recommendation	8	17

TABLE B.3
LEVEL OF DOCUMENTATION OF KNOWLEDGE
ASSERTIONS BY DATE OF POLICY STATEMENT

Type of Support	Number of policy statements with given level of documentation as highest level	
	1983 and earlier	Post 1983
No knowledge statement	11	3
Vaguely documented	6	6
Informal specific documentation	3	8
Bibliographic citation	5	6

$X^2 = 6.79$, $df = 3$, $p > .10$

of a political process (National Association of Social Workers, 1988). Certainly they are an expression of the social work profession's values and they reflect the profession's knowledge beliefs.

But values and unsubstantiated knowledge beliefs are not compelling in social policy discussions with those who have different values and different beliefs. When values confront contrary values, resolution of the conflict lies either in persuasion by appeal to superordinate values or in the use of power to enforce value supremacy. When beliefs about the nature of reality confront contrary beliefs, resolution of the conflict lies either in appeal to empirical evidence or in the use of power to enforce action in accordance with a given set of beliefs.

The social work profession does not at present have the power to impose either its values or its beliefs about the nature of reality onto the larger society. Indeed, social work's very values would perhaps prohibit any attempt at such even if it did have the power. Thus, social work must use persuasion in social policy discussions.

Social work as a profession may be highly self-conscious about its values, but it has no monopoly on values. It is proper to display one's special set of values as social work does in *Social Work Speaks* (National Association of Social Workers, 1988). However, it might be more effective in the social policy arena for social work to de-emphasize the specialness of its values and seek consensus with others in grounding its values in superordinate values with greater general acceptance.

In assessing the state of reality and in proposing actions to bring about a more highly valued state of reality, social work must, in order to be more persuasive, depend to a greater degree on objectively verified knowledge, rather than subjectively held beliefs. The principal way of distinguishing between the two is by use of formal citations to the sources that document the verification of the knowledge statements. When verified knowledge is insufficient to guide policy recommendations, this should be admitted and additional research should be recommended to produce the required objectively verified knowledge. Briar (1981) has argued that the absence of a research-generated knowledge base and of vigorous efforts to expand it will, in the long run, erode the social work profession's credibility outside the profession.

We have seen above that the social work profession in speaking to social policy does not appear at present to value highly objectively verified knowledge. Data regarding other service professions' use of knowledge as a basis for policy recommendations is not available to provide a direct comparison between social work and other professions on-this characteristic. Nevertheless, social work appears to give less emphasis to the results of empirical research as a guide to general professional practice than do some other human service professions (Austin, 1991; Simpson, 1978). The low value that social work places on research-based knowledge is still the case despite a generation of lip service to the importance of research; and in spite of social work education mandating exposure to the research process in professional education. Both the formal socialization of professional education and the informal socialization of professional organizations would seem to have failed in the inculcation of a valuing of objectively verified knowledge as the basis of professional practice recommendations.

Social work has much to offer to the social policy arena; its values impel it to improve the human condition and its professional activities provide it with the opportunity to develop knowledge based on the actual human condition. In order to most effectively carry out its mission, the profession must better document its knowledge beliefs, especially those which are made public, so that it will more likely be heard by those it must influence both within and outside the profession.

REFERENCES

Austin, D. (1991). Comments on research development in social work (Commentary). *Social Work Research and Abstracts, 27*, 38-41.

Bartlett, H.M. (1958). Toward clarification and improvement of social work practice. *Social Work, 3*, 39.

Bartlett, H.M. (1970). *The common base of social work practice.* New York: National Association of Social Workers.

Briar, S. (1981). The project on research utilization in social work education. In S. Briar, H. Weissman & A. Rubin (Eds.). *Research utilization in social work education* (pp. 1-5). New York: Council on Social Work Education.

Council on Social Work Education. (1982). *Curriculum policy for the master's degree and baccalaureate degree programs in social work education.* New York: Author.

Council on Social Work Education. (1988). *Handbook: of accreditation standards and procedures.* Washington, DC: Author.

Glisson, C. (1983, October). *Trends in social work research: Substantive and methodological implications for doctoral curricula.* Presentation at the Annual Meeting, Group For the Advancement of Doctoral Education, School of Social Work, The University of Alabama, Tuscaloosa, AL.

Glisson, C. (1990). *Trends in social work research: 1977-1988.* Report prepared for the Task Force on Social Work Research, National Institute for Mental Health.

Gordon, W.E. (1962). A critique of the working definition. *Social Work, 7*, 3-13.

Greenwood, E. (1957). Social work research: A decade of reappraisal. *Social Service Review, 31*, 311-320.

Hartman, A. (1990). Many ways of knowing (Editorial). *Social Work, 35*, 3-4.

Jayaratne, S. (1979). Analysis of selected social work journals and productivity rankings among schools of social work. *Journal of Education for Social Work, 15*, 72-80.

Kahn, A.J. (1954). The nature of social work knowledge. In C. Kasius (Ed.), *New directions in social work* (pp. 194-214). New York: Harper.

Karger, H. J. (1983). Science, research, and social work: Who controls the profession? *Social Work, 28*, 200-205.

Kirk, S.A. & Fischer, J. (1976). Do social workers understand research? *Journal of Education for Social Work, 12*, 63-70.

Lewis, H. L. (1982). *The intellectual base of social work practice.* New York: Haworth.

National Association of Social Workers. (1964). *Building social work knowledge.* New York: Author.

National Association of Social Workers. (1988). *Social work speaks.* Silver Spring, MD: Author.

Simpson, R.L. (1978). Is research utilization for social workers? *Journal of Social Service Research, 2,* 143-157.

Taber, M. & Shapiro, I. (1965). Social work and its knowledge base: A content analysis of the periodical literature. *Social Work, 10,* 100-106.

Task Force on Social Work Research. (1988). *Information summary.* Austin, TX: Author.

Weick, A. (1987). Reconceptualizing the philosophical perspective of social work. *Social Service Review, 61,* 218-230.

Weinberger, R. & Tripodi, T. (1969). Trends in types of research reported in selected social work journals, 1956-65. *Social Service Review, 43,* 439-447.

Williams, L.F. & Hopps, J.G. (1987). Publication as a practice goal: Enhancing opportunities for social workers. *Social Work, 32,* 373-376.

Williams, L. F., & Hopps, J. G. (1988). On the nature of professional communication: Publication for practitioners. *Social Work, 33,* 453-459.

Research Study C

DECIMATING GENERAL ASSISTANCE:
ITS IMPACT ON THE RELATIONSHIPS OF THE POOR

Anthony P. Halter

The Pennsylvania Welfare Reform Act of 1982 provides that the able-bodied General Assistance population may receive cash assistance for a maximum of 90 days in any twelve-month period. This study describes the experiences of a segment of those who were discontinued from general assistance as a result of the Pennsylvania changes and who tuned to family and friends for support.

SINCE 1991, ECONOMIC AND FISCAL CONSTRAINTS have caused some state governments and local municipalities to reduce or discontinue their general assistance programs. According to the Center on Budget and Policy Priorities (1991), state general assistance cash welfare programs were hit harder in 1991 than any other type of low income program. The states and localities that have discontinued or reduced their programs include: Arizona, Connecticut, Illinois, Kansas, Maine, Massachusetts, Michigan, Minnesota, New Mexico, New York, Ohio, Rhode Island, Washington, the District of Columbia, and San Diego County, California (Center on Social Welfare Policy and Law, 1992). General assistance (GA) programs are state and/or locally funded; legislation and eligibility requirements are set by the individual states. When state budgets are stretched as a result of economic slowdowns, general assistance is an area subject to reduction or termination. These recent changes will have acute effects during the present recession (Center on Budget and Policy Priorities, 1991), and human service advocates have voiced concern about their limited resources for those who are discontinued and who do not find employment.

Numerous articles have reviewed the impact of welfare reform on individuals receiving Aid to Families with Dependent Children (Axinn & Stem, 1987; Bradbury, Danziger, Smolensky, & Smolensky, 1979; Chandler & Williams, 1989; Coughlin, 1989; Dear, 1989; Ellwood, 1988; United States General Accounting Office, 1988; Glass, 1982; Goodwin, 1989; Mason, Wodarski, & Parham, 1985; Pearce, 1978; Rein, 1982; Rovner, 1991; Spakes, 1982; United States Committee on Government Operations, 1985; Wallace & Long, 1987). There has been, however, a limited number of studies on general assistance (Halter, 1989; Stagner & Richman, 1986). Early reports of the termination of Michigan's general assistance program indicate that most of those who are discontinued move in with relatives or friends, and that non-profit and voluntary agencies such as shelters and food pantries are providing services to those who remain unemployed (Sylvester, 1992). Studies describing the impact of previous changes in general assistance programs may make a valuable contribution by assessing the effects of these present changes and determining what future research is needed to measure the outcome of these reductions. This article reviews the experiences of a group of individuals who were discontinued from general assistance in Pennsylvania, the impact discontinuance had on their relationships with relatives and friends, and also describes their dependence on other agencies such as shelters for the homeless.

WELFARE REFORM STRATEGY IN PENNSYLVANIA

IN 1980, SOME STATE GOVERNORS and the Reagan Administration were concerned that the amount of funds allocated for welfare programs had increased to the point where the system was neither cost-effective nor capable of helping those most in need (Sugarman, Bass, & Beinecke, 1982). To rectify this, a sharper line was drawn between those who could work and those who were classified as "truly needy" and entitled to welfare, in the belief that this would motivate the able-bodied poor to work their way out of poverty.

The objective of these measures was to reduce costs and decrease caseloads by removing recipients from the welfare rolls as quickly as possible. Pennsylvania's Governor Richard Thomburgh espoused a similar philosophy, believing that general assistance encouraged dependence by providing an alternative to work (Commonwealth of Pennsylvania House of Representatives, 1982). In 1982, the Governor signed the Pennsylvania Welfare Reform Act, which divided General Assistance recipients into two groups: the chronically needy and the transitionally needy. The chronically needy were entitled to general assistance as long as they fit the established criteria, while the transitionally needy, those between the ages of 18 and 45 and considered able to work (able-bodied), were eligible for general assistance cash benefits for only ninety days in any twelve-month period (Commonwealth of Pennsylvania, Status, 1982).

Since 1982, other states have followed Pennsylvania's example by either discontinuing general assistance or placing a time constraint on the able-bodied welfare population. Louisiana (1986), Arkansas (1987), and Oklahoma (1986) discontinued their general assistance programs for able-bodied individuals (Lewin I. & James Bell Associates, 1990), while in July of 1990, Montana limited employable persons on general assistance to four months of assistance in any 12-month period.

Bakke (1933) showed that men who remained unemployed over extended periods of time could not rely on family members for financial and psychological support since family members were experiencing similar difficulties. As the means of subsistence changed, the individuals' relationships disintegrated. Shuart and Lewko (1988), while studying welfare recipients who were looking for work, found that family members often viewed joblessness as personal failure. Therefore, this author expected that those who were discontinued from cash assistance would initially turn to their relatives or close friends for support, thereby placing additional stress and pressure on them. This study describes the experiences of a sample of the Pennsylvania general assistance population who turned to family and friends for support after general assistance benefits were terminated.

METHODOLOGY

A QUALITATIVE RESEARCH APPROACH was used for this study. Specific open-ended questions were asked in order to allow for the elaboration of comments, and to clarify the respondents' attitudes and concerns. The sample consisted of forty-one individuals who were discontinued from general assistance. Fifty names and addresses of individuals from Philadelphia were randomly selected by the Pennsylvania Department of Public Welfare from those who had been discontinued from general assistance. Forty-one individuals were contacted. Nine potential respondents could not be found. All respondents had been without welfare from four to six months. The respondents were interviewed in person at shelters or by telephone during the fall and winter of 1987 and the spring of 1988.

Four areas were included in the study: identifying the job-seeking behaviors exhibited by the population, determining whether those who were discontinued turned to their families or close friends, describing the changes that took place in relationships with family and friends, and assessing whether the person who was discontinued turned to other agencies such as public or privately-operated shelters for support. Since the discontinuance was based on the theory that this population could find work, employability and employment opportunities for this population were studied. The specific questions included:

- What were the demographics of the respondents based on race, age and sex'?

- What were the educational levels of the respondents studied?

- Of the respondents studied, how many found jobs?

- What was the hourly rate of those who found jobs?

- What difficulties did the respondents have in finding jobs?

- What types of jobs were found by the respondents?

- What health problems were experienced by the respondents?

- How frequently have respondents relied on family or friends for help?

- When on welfare, who supported the respondents?

- Who supported the respondents after welfare was discontinued?

- Did the respondents depend more on family members now than before discontinuance?

- Have relationships with the respondents' relatives improved, deteriorated, or remained the same?

- Did relationships with the respondents' friends improve, deteriorate, or remain the same after discontinuance?

- Did the respondents use other public or private agencies more after discontinuance?

RESULTS

OF THE RESPONDENTS WHO WERE INTERVIEWED, 49% were Caucasian, 40% African-American, and 11% Latino-American. Seventy-one percent of the respondents were male and 29% were female. In terms of age, 21% were between the ages of 18 to 25, 42% were between 26 and 32, 28% were between 33 and 40, and 9% were between 40 and 45. Sixty-six percent were high school drop-outs,

TABLE C.1
QUESTION: WHAT TYPE OF JOB
DID YOU FIND?

Answer	N	%
Laborer	8	50.0
Fast-Food	4	25.0
Janitor	2	12.5
Domestic	1	6.25
Machinist	1	6.25

24% had completed high school, and 10% had attended college for periods ranging from a few months to three years.

Thirty-nine percent of the respondents found jobs, and 61% remained unemployed. Table C.1 points out that these jobs included employment as fast-food restaurant worker, laborer, nurse's aide, and janitor. The average hourly rate was $5.15 per hour and was determined by adding the hourly rates of the respondents who found work and dividing by the number of respondents (16) in that group.

Prior to discontinuance, 61% were living in their own apartments, 22% were living in single rooms, and 17% were living with friends, or relatives. When interviewed, 29% were living in shelters, while 64% were living either with relatives or friends, and 7% were living alone. For the 29% who were living in shelters job-finding became more difficult, since many local employers knew that the address given on the job application was a shelter and were reluctant to hire homeless individuals. One individual stated, "As every day goes by, looking for work gets harder and you look at yourself like a loser. I use shelters a lot; at least you get fed."

Those living with friends or in shelters reported physical health problems they had not experienced when they lived independently. Of those in this situation, 41% stated they had health problems that included respiratory infections, pneumonia, and lice infestation. Mental health problems such as depression and extreme anxiety were reported by 37% of the respondents. Of those living with relatives or alone, 20% mentioned having physical health problems that included stomach problems and difficulty sleeping, while 32% stated that they had high anxiety and depression.

The author expected reliance on relatives or friends to be the first means of support the respondents would turn to after discontinuance. Therefore, determining the extent of this reliance was one of the areas that was investigated initially.

Reliance on Relatives and Friends

Because of a need for financial support, housing, and food, relationships with others played an important role in the lives of those who were discontinued. Table C.2 shows that 68% of the respondents indicated that they relied more frequently on family and friends after discontinuance, while 17% stated that their reliance on others was about the same, and 15% state that they relied less frequently. One respondent stated, "I'm always on the move, trying to make ends meet. Hustling, part-time work when you can get it, or unloading something on

TABLE C.2

QUESTION: COMPARED TO WHEN YOU
WERE ON WELFARE, HOW FREQUENTLY
HAVE YOU HAD TO RELY ON YOUR
FAMILY OR FRIENDS FOR HELP?

Answer	N	%
More Frequently	28	68
The Same	7	17
Less Frequently	6	15

TABLE C.3

UESTION: WHO HELPED YOU TO
GET BY WHEN YOU WERE ON WELFARE?

Answer	N	%
Nobody, just welfare	33	80
Relatives and Friends	6	15
Part-time work and welfare	2	5

TABLE C.4

QUESTION: AFTER DISCONTINUANCE OF
WELFARE, WHO HELPED YOU TO GET BY?

Answer	N	%
Nobody	3	7
Friends	2	5
Relatives and Friends	9	22
Private Agencies	2	5
Friends, Relatives and Private Agencies	25	61

the street."

Table C.3 indicates that while on welfare, 80% of the respondents stated that they received help from no one, while 15% stated that they relied upon friends and welfare for support, and 5% pointed out that they managed with a combination of part-time work and welfare.

However, Table C.4 demonstrates that after discontinuance of welfare, 93% of the respondents depended on friends, relatives, and public and private agencies such as food pantries, shelters, community mental health centers, and the Salvation Army.

Impact on Relatives

This phase describes changes that occurred in the familial relationships of the respondents. Initially, those who were discontinued and who could not find jobs tuned to family members for support. Table C.5 points out that at the time of the

TABLE C.5
QUESTION: DO YOU DEPEND MORE ON FAMILY
MEMBERS NOW THAN BEFORE DISCONTINUANCE?

Answer	N	%
Don't depend on relatives	11	27
Depend more on relatives	5	12
Depend more on relatives, but it is difficult	9	22
First depended on relatives but gradually became dependent on other sources	8	20
Depend about the same	5	12
Depend less on them	3	7

interview, 12% depended more on their families after discontinuance and 22% stated that they depended more on their relatives now than before being discontinued but the living situation was stressful. In addition, 20% of the respondents indicated that although they had relied on their relatives initially, they now depended more on friends, private or public agencies, or shelters. Also, 27% stated that they did not depend on relatives, while 7% indicated that they depended less on relatives than previously.

Based on the comments made, it appears that discontinuance generated tension and hardship among family members. As Table C.6 indicates, 53% referred to additional pressure at home or having to leave the household. In all instances, family members included sisters, brothers, mothers, and fathers, but not husbands or wives. One individual stated, "For awhile, right after I was cut off, I stayed with my mom and dad, but I didn't want to be a burden, so I left." Another pointed out, "You lose relatives when you're put in this situation." There were no reports of violence or abuse resulting from the tension caused by lack of funds. However, 12% mentioned that if they had stayed in their households, violence could have occurred.

Impact on Friends

Another important phase in the cycle of dependence of the transitionally needy was evident in their relationships with friends. One respondent stated, "Now, I don't have friends. When you need friends, most turn their back on you. The only friends I have are the ones who are in the same situation as me." Table C.7 indicates that 36.5% of the respondents stated that relationships with friends had gotten worse since discontinuance, 17% reported that relationships had changed or that they no longer had any friends, and 14.5% indicated that their only friendships were now with people who were in the same situation. Thirty-two percent of the respondents indicated that friendships had remained the same.

When asked if they had sought assistance from private or public agencies at some time after discontinuance, 85% answered affirmatively and 15% negatively. When asked if they found it necessary to use these agencies more, less, or the same amount compared to when they had been on welfare, 76% indicated that they used shelters more than before, while 7% stated that they used them the same amount, and 17% indicated that they were seeking

TABLE C.6
QUESTION: HAVE YOUR RELATIONSHIPS WITH
RELATIVES GOTTEN BETTER, WORSE, OR REMAINED THE SAME?

Answer	N	%
Things have not really changed.	4	10
There are additional pressures and tensions because of problems in getting along with family members.	12	29
I had to leave my relatives.	10	24
The family was helping me.	5	13
I do not have a family life.	10	24

assistance less frequently.

The financial hardships brought on by the discontinuance of general assistance placed additional pressure on the respondents' relationships. When they were discontinued from general assistance, most of the respondents managed by depending on a system of networks that consisted of family, friends, and private agencies. In discussions with the respondents at shelters, they often regarded other residents as their only friends. A typical comment made by those individuals was that they felt that they were invisible. That is, they were not really seen by others on the streets, and they felt that they had "fallen through the cracks." One respondent stated that "Nobody gives a damn about me. Walking to work they just see right through you."

DISCUSSION

AFTER DISCONTINUANCE OF CASH ASSISTANCE, the individual would continue to look for work, and if unable to find a job, would initially turn to relatives. Although these individuals were classified as employable, 61% could not find work. Based on the comments made by the respondents, reliance on relatives, friends, and shelters increased after discontinuance of general assistance.

Although the responsibility of relatives is not a legal issue, the consequence of the Pennsylvania Welfare Reform Act is that some families did assume support of a sister, brother, son, or daughter who has been discontinued. This included providing funds, shelter, or food which eventually led to the respondent leaving the household and turning to friends, shelters, or both.

Michigan is an example of one state that has discontinued general assistance. Shelter directors in Detroit reported in November, 1991 that all shelters in the city were filled and that some were turning individuals away. A weakened economy and limited state funds have caused many state governors to consider a quick-fix approach to addressing the problem of budget deficits by reducing or discontinuing general assistance.

However, eliminating individuals from welfare with the understanding that they can find work at a time of limited job availability may serve to necessitate institutional relief in the disguise of shelters and require some relatives to be placed in a more difficult financial situation by having to provide for those who are discontinued from general assistance. Other agencies may also be required to take on the responsibility of servicing this population. This is best exemplified by a review of the increase of shelter activity in Philadelphia after general assis-

TABLE C.7

QUESTION: HAVE YOUR RELATIONSHIPS WITH FRIENDS GOTTEN
BETTER, WORSE, OR REMAINED THE SAME AFTER DISCONTINUANCE?

Answer	N	%
Remained the same	13	32.0
Now have no friends	7	17.0
Relationship with friends have gotten worse	15	36.5
Relationship with friends have changed and new friends are those who are in the same situation	6	14.5

tance reductions were made. Prior to enactment of the general assistance reductions in Philadelphia, the total nights of shelter use (length of stay multiplied by number of people) was 6,525; by 1984 and after enactment, the number had risen to 22,687 (Katz, 1986).

RECOMMENDATIONS FOR SOCIAL WORKERS

Proactive planning by state governments is necessary to determine whether reductions in public welfare programs may result in increased costs for families and private and non-profit institutions in the future. Social workers should evaluate the systemic effects of these reductions on families and institutions. Shelters, food banks, mental health centers, and non-profit agencies should maintain data concerning the victims of these reductions. In addition, data should be kept on those poor families who are attempting to support relatives who have been discontinued from general assistance.

Additional steps social workers can take in order to address these changes include:

- Evaluate the impact of the changes on individuals, families, and agencies.

- Determine whether the proposed savings these changes may generate will increase demands on homeless programs, emergency food programs, relatives and friends.

- Provide training for advocates and social workers in acquiring information about the impact of the changes on relatives, friends and agencies.

- Become familiar with the changes in procedures and policies in order to educate individuals who are most at risk, as well as their families and friends.

- Provide training for advocates and social workers in evaluation, testimony, and the present general assistance legislation.

- Develop alliances with other groups that support maintaining the present general assistance program and with individuals, academics, advocates, and legislators who are familiar with recent policy changes.

The intent of the Welfare Reform Act of 1982 was to eliminate a portion of the able-bodied population from welfare with the understanding that they were employable and would ultimately find jobs. However, most of the respondents were unable to find permanent employment that enabled them to become financially independent. The ultimate effect of this law may be that it serves to create additional hardship among the poor and place additional strain on their families and friends, and on private and public agencies such as shelters and food pantries.

REFERENCES

Axinn, J. & Stem, M. (1987). Women and the post-industrial welfare state. *Social Work 32,* 282-286.

Bakke, E.W. (1933). *The unemployed man.* New York: Nisbett.

Bradbury, K., Danziger, S., Smolensky, E., & Smolensky, P. (1979). Public assistance, female headship and economic well-being. *Journal of Marriage and the Family, 8,* 519-535.

Center on Budget and Policy Priorities. (1991). *The states and the poor: How budget decisions in 1991 affected low income people.* Washington, D.C.: Author.

Center on Social Welfare Policy and Law. (1992, February). *1991: The poor got poorer as welfare programs were slashed.* New York City: Author. (Publication No. 165)

Chandler, S. & Williams, J. (1989). Family structures and the feminization of poverty: Women in Hawaii. *Journal of Sociology and Social Welfare, 16,* 205-222.

Commonwealth of Pennsylvania House of Representatives. (1982). *Report to the state house of representatives health and welfare committee on the impact of act 75.* Harrisburg, Pennsylvania: Commonwealth of Pennsylvania Health and Welfare Committee.

Commonwealth of Pennsylvania. (1982). *Welfare reform and jobs development: A budget and policy brief.* Harrisburg, Pennsylvania: Governor's Office.

Commonwealth of Pennsylvania. (1982). *Status report.* Harrisburg, Pennsylvania: Governor's Office.

Coughlin, R. (1989). *Reforming welfare: Lessons, limits, and choices.* New Mexico: University of New Mexico Press.

Dear, R. (1989). What's right with welfare? The other face of AFDC. *Journal of Sociology and Social Welfare, 16,* 5-44.

Ellwood, D. (1988). *Poor support: Poverty in the American family.* New York: Basic Books, Inc.

Glass, B. (1982). Comparing employed and unemployed welfare recipients: A discriminant analysis. *Journal of Sociology and Social Welfare, 9,* 19-36.

Goodwin, L. (1989). The work incentive program in current perspective: What have we learned? Where do we go from here? *Journal of Sociology and Social Welfare, 16,* 45-66.

Halter, A. (1989). Welfare reform: One state's alterative. *Journal of Sociology and Social Welfare, 16,* 151-162.

Katz, M. (1986). *In the shadow of' the poorhouse: A social history of Welfare in America.* New York: Basic Books, Inc.

Lewin I. & James Bell Associates. (1990, August). *Characteristics of General Assistance programs 1989.* Washington, D.C. Health and Science International, Inc.

Mason, J., Wodarski, J.S., & Parham, T. (1985). Work and Welfare: A reevaluation of AFDC. *Social Work, 30,* 197-203.

Pearce, D. (1978). The feminization of poverty: Women, work and welfare. *Urban and Social Change Review, 11,* 28-36.

Rein, M. (1982). Work in welfare: Past failures and future strategies. *Social Service Review, 56,* 211-229.

Rovner, J. (1991). Beyond the dole. *Governing: The States and Localities, 4,* 19-22.

Shuart, V., & Lewko, J. (1988). Exposure of young welfare recipients to family and peer receipt of welfare and unemployment benefits. *Journal of Sociology and Social Welfare, 15,* 73-86.

Spakes, P. (1982). Mandatory work registration for welfare parents: A family impact analysis. *Journal of Marriage and Family, 44,* 685-699.

Stagner, M. & Richman, H. (1986). Reexamining the role of general assistance. *Public Welfare, 44,* 26-42.

Sugarman, J., Bass, G., & Beinecke, R. (1982). *The Reagan budget.* Washington, DC: The Human Services Information Center.

Sylvester, K. (1992). The easiest welfare cut. *Governing: The States and Localities, 5,* 24-26.

United States General Accounting Office. (1988). *Work and welfare analysis of AFDC employment programs in four states.* Washington, D.C.: General Accounting Office.

United States Committee On Government Operations. (1985). *Barriers to self-sufficiency for single female heads of families.* Washington, D.C.: United States Government Printing Office.

Wallace, J. & Long, D. (1987). *GAIN: Planning and early implementation.* New York: The Manpower Demonstration Research Corporation.

Research Study D

SEXUAL ADJUSTMENT FOLLOWING SPINAL CORD INJURY: EMPIRICAL FINDINGS AND CLINICAL IMPLICATIONS

Romel W. Mackelprang and Dean H. Hepworth

The psychosocial and sexual adjustments of people with spinal cord injuries have long been considered by health care professionals to be intertwined; however, research to substantiate these beliefs is sparse. This article reports the findings of a study (a) comparing pre-injury to post-injury sexual interest and activity, (b) assessing reasons for reduced sexual activity in respondents who reported diminished sexual behaviors, and (c) comparing the social and emotional adjustments of those with reduced activity to people reporting similar or increased sexual contact. Resultant data documented the critical relationship between psychosocial and sexual adjustment. Practice implications and suggestions are discussed.

EACH YEAR IN THE UNITED STATES, approximately 10,000 persons survive acute spinal cord injury (SCI) but are rendered paraplegic or quadriplegic (Trieschmann, 1980). Of 9,647 persons treated at 19 regional SCI centers from 1973 to 1985, 51.1% were discharged with complete lesions, blocking all voluntary function below the level of injury, while only 1.1% left with complete recovery (Spinal Cord Injury, 1986).

Following discharge from the hospital, persons with SCI face drastically altered lives. A wheelchair substitutes for legs to provide mobility. Voluntary bowel and bladder control are lost, and incontinence is prevented only with proper care and management. Frequently, medical and physical complications, such as skin problems and pain, severely limit activity level. People with quadriplegia may require physical assistance moving from bed to wheelchair, and in dressing, bathing, and even eating (Bedbrook, 1981).

Many emotional and social problems typically follow the physical changes precipitated by SCI. Common initial emotional difficulties include depression, mourning, and anxiety. Feelings of loss of control over the body and environment frequently occur (Pervin-Dixon, 1988). Fear seems to be commonly experienced as persons face an uncertain future. A major focus of these fears is future sexual functioning (Woodbury & Redd, 1987; Novak & Mitchell, 1988).

Many authors have investigated sexual interest, activity, and problems following SCI; however, little has been written on the relationship between sexual activity and overall social and emotional adjustment. The purposes of this article, therefore are (a) to discuss the effects of SCI on sexual functioning, (b) to report the findings of a study designed to explore the relationship between sexual activity and social and emotional adjustment, and (c) to discuss interventions we can use to assist people with their sexual adjustments.

EFFECTS OF SPINAL CORD INJURY ON SEXUAL FUNCTIONING

SEXUAL FUNCTIONING is significantly altered following SCI. Sensation and movement are impaired, and the ability to be physically expressive is limited. Because genital functioning is controlled through the lowest part of the spinal cord (sacral segments 2, 3, and 4), anyone with SCI is at risk of sexual impairment. In addition to sensory and mobility loss, men experience erectile and fertility problems. As Guttman (1976) stated, "Normal sexual function depends on a coordinated activity of cerebral, spinal, and peripheral components of the nervous system as well as ... the reproductive organs themselves" (p. 474). When this coordinated activity is impaired, as in SCI, sexual problems arise (Szasz, 1986; Masters, Johnson, & Kolodny, 1985).

Based on their review of several studies that included an aggregate total of 2,252 spinal cord injured men, Griffith, Tomko, and Timms (1973) reported that from 54% to 87% of the men had erectile abilities, however, not all men with erectile capabilities were able to engage in intercourse because erections were too short in duration, were inconsistent, and/or lacked firmness. Most erections were reflexogenic, occurring not because of psychic input from the brain, but from sensory nerve impulses originating through the spinal cord with nerves controlling blood supply to the penis, thus producing an erection. Psychogenic erections, which occur in response to erotic stimuli, were much less common. Data regarding incident of coitus were as follows: 8% to 82% attempted intercourse, and only 5% to 50% were successful. From 2% to 14% of the men experienced orgasm. Ejaculation occurred in only 3% to 20% of the subjects, whereas from 0% to 5% sired children.

In general, three factors affect sexual functioning of males with SCI. First, people with incomplete cord lesions retain a higher degree of genital function than those with complete cord injuries. Second, men with higher level cord lesions and upper motor neuron lesions have higher frequencies of erections and coitus. Finally, those with lower level cord lesions have higher rates of fertility and incidence of orgasm (Griffith et al., 1973).

Although the literature concerning female sexual functioning after SCI is sparse, available information indicates that menstruation, if interrupted, resumes within a few months of injury (Treischmann, 1980). The ability of women to engage in most sex acts seems unimpaired. Fertility is generally unimpaired, and women who choose to have children are usually able to deliver vaginally (Mackelprang & McDonald, 1988; Rossier, Ruffieux, & Ziegler, 1969). However, women who become pregnant and carry the pregnancy to term risk complications such as urinary tract infections, pressure sores, and autonomic dysreflexia. Thus, their need for proper health care is critical (McGregor & Meeuwsen, 1985).

Sexual arousal for men and women who have lost tactile sensation in the genitals can occur in several ways. Stimulation of secondary erogenous zones, such as the lips, ears, neck, and breasts can be very arousing. Sexual satisfaction can also derive from contributing to and participating in the pleasure one's partner is receiving as well as from seeing the genitals fondled (Mackelprang & McDonald, 1988; Thornton, 1981). Some people with no genital sensation even report having orgasms, which they often experience more emotionally than physically. Such orgasms tend to be associated with increased muscle and sexual tension followed by profound muscle relaxation, decreased respiration, heart rate, and drowsiness (Hohmann, 1973).

SEXUAL ADJUSTMENT FOLLOWING SPINAL CORD INJURY

ALTHOUGH THE PHYSICAL CHANGES produced by SCI are emotionally traumatic, anxiety about the effects of the disability on sexual functioning can be as threatening as the disability itself (Hohmann, 1975). Many fear they will be unable to provide pleasure or will be rejected as sexual partners. Others, due to lack of genital sensation, question whether they will be able to enjoy sex. The fear of bowel and bladder incontinence can be overwhelming to still others (Szasz, 1986).

Sexuality education and counseling have maximum impact when implemented as an integral part of an SCI rehabilitation program and can assist patients and their partners to meet physical challenges and to enjoy sexual intimacy. Though sexual experiences are usually uncomfortable initially, with adequate knowledge and persistence, patients can usually achieve satisfying sexual relationships (Bregman & Hadley, 1976; Mackelprang & McDonald, 1988). Without adequate preparation, serious sexual problems can develop. For example, David, Gur & Rozin (1977) interviewed women who had married men with SCI and found that a great source of dissatisfaction was their husbands' infertility, a problem of which they often were not aware prior to marriage.

Sexual adjustment is an evolving process after SCI. With time and effort, the discomfort experienced during sexual intimacy lessens, and sex becomes more enjoyable (Fitting, Salisbury, Davies, & Mayclin, 1978). Interest in sex generally remains high and research indicates that sexuality is an integral part of overall adjustment of people with SCI. Women seem to have good long-range adjustment (Bregman & Hadley, 1976; Fitting et al., 1978; Ray & West, 1984), whereas men seem to have more difficulty (Berkman, Weissman, & Friedlich, 1978; Phelps et al., 1983; Ray & West, 1984). This may be due in part to greater functional physical losses for men in erectile capability, ejaculation, and fertility, or it may be that some women are more responsive to the range of physical sexual expression and focus less on genital stimulation than men.

Even with all the physical limitations, many people are able to enjoy satisfying sex lives. Sex is different following spinal cord injury, but not necessarily inferior. In this regard, Trieschmann (1980) stated:

> If we are going to study sexual function in men and women with SCI, we must broaden our focus to include the multitude of sex acts that form a pattern of communication between two caring people, rather than persisting in focusing exclusively on sex acts that are motoric and genital. We must begin to view sexual function as encompassing more than sexual intercourse only. (p. 134)

THE STUDY

To EXPAND KNOWLEDGE of the relationship between sexual activity and social and emotional adjustment following SCI, a study was designed to gather and analyze follow-up data on patients who had been hospitalized for treatment of paraplegia or quadriplegia. Subjects were asked to compare both their post-SCI sexual interest and activity to pre-injury interest and activity. From subjects who reported reduced sexual activity, data were then gathered on reasons for this decrease. Contrasts were made between subjects who reported reduced sexual activity, and those who reported similar or increased sexual activity on several social and emotional adjustment variables.

The Sample

Subjects for this study were drawn from a population of 115 patients who had received a minimum of three weeks of rehabilitation for acute spinal cord injuries at the University of Utah Spinal Cord Injury Center between June 1980 and December 1985. Only people with traumatic injuries were included. To avoid confounding of variables, people with SCI resulting from diseases such as multiple sclerosis, cancer, or transverse myelitis were excluded from the study. In addition, people with significant secondary diagnoses such as head injury or preexisting mental retardation were excluded for the same reasons. To be included in the study, subjects must have experienced significant alterations in sexual functioning, bowel and bladder functioning, and/or mobility.

Of the 115 original subjects, three died, 16 could not be located, and 15 declined to be interviewed. Some of those who declined participation expressed a willingness to be involved, but after a minimum of three unsuccessful interview attempts, they were dropped from the study. The resultant 81 subjects were interviewed between March and June 1986. Fifty-three had paraplegia, and 28 had quadriplegia. Time elapsed between injury and interview ranged from six months to six years.

Instruments and Data Collection

Data from the large majority of clients were gathered through telephone interviews conducted by the senior author or by a second-year graduate social work student, whose practicum placement was in the hospital's Division of Physical Medicine and Rehabilitation. The student was extensively trained and supervised throughout the study. All respondents were familiar with the setting, which contributed to the favorable 84% response rate of subjects contacted. Several subjects, in fact, were interviewed in person during social visits they were making to the hospital. Three separate instruments were employed for collecting data as follows:

1. An interview schedule consisting of 39 questions was developed and used to gather demographic data, including marital status as well as information regarding level and severity of injury, physical and medical problems, physical assistance needed, and sexual activity. The instrument was pretested for relevance and clarity on professional colleagues with SCI and was refined before being employed with actual respondents.
2. The General Well-Being Schedule (GWBS) was used to assess respondents' subjective feelings of well-being and distress. The GWBS, developed by the Department of Health, Education and Welfare, National Center for Health Statistics, consists of 33 close-ended questions and is relatively brief and easy to administer. It yields a score on 'overall well-being' and has six subscales that tap various aspects of well-being which are as follows: (a) feelings of energy, (b) freedom from health concerns, (c) relaxed vs. anxious mood, (d) emotional control, (e) cheerful vs. depressed mood, and (f) life interest and satisfaction. The GWBS was particularly valuable because unlike related instruments, it measures well-being rather than focusing only on problem feelings. The GWBS has been extensively tested and found to be reliable and valid (Fazio, 1977).
3. The Interview Schedule for Social Interaction (ISSI) was administered to

assess the support systems and social interactions of respondents. This instrument contains 52 items, several of which include sub-items. An advantage of the ISSI over other instruments used to assess social support is that it measures not only availability of social relationships, but also respondents' perceptions of the adequacy of available relationships.

The ISSI yields data on the following four major scales: (a) Availability of Attachment (AVAT) to relatives, close friends, and others in a person's social network; (b) Adequacy of Attachment (ADAT), which measures a persons's perceptions of the extent to which attachments accurately match their social needs; (c) Availability of Social Integration (AVSI), which measures available opportunities for integration into various types of social activities and organizations; and (d) Adequacy of Social Integration (ADSI), which measures subjective perceptions of the extent to which social interaction meets individual needs. As the ADAT scale is variable from respondent to respondent, an alternative measure, Adequacy of Attachment Percentage (ADATPC) was developed to provide a measure based on the percentage ADAT questions the respondent is asked. As the score of ADAT is partly dependent on responses to AVAT, ADATPC is considered "logically superior" to ADAT and therefore is often used in lieu of ADAT (Henderson, Byme, & DuncanJones, 1981).

In addition to the major scales, the ISSI has 12 minor subscales that yield measures of various aspects of social adjustment. Developed in Australia, the ISSI has been tested vigorously and determined to be a reliable and valid instrument (Henderson, Duncan-Jones, Byme, & Scott, 1980).

FINDINGS

OF THE 81 RESPONDENTS, 24 were female and 57 were male. Twenty-three respondents were married at the time of injury, and 25 were married at the time of interview. Three subjects reported they were living with a lover at the time of the study. Six respondents reported they had divorced following injury, four had separated from their spouses, and eight reported they had married. There had been no changes in the marital status of 60 respondents. The mean age of the respondents at the time of the interview was 29.7 years. Time elapsed between injury and interview ranged from six months to six years, with a mean of 3.1 years.

Differences in Sexual Interest and Activity Between Men and Women

Virtually no differences were found in sexual interest between men and women. When asked to compare pre-injury sexual interest to present interest, 25% of the women reported reduced sexual interest, 50% reported no change, and 25% stated their interest in sex had increased. Comparisons for men were as follows: 24.6% experienced reduced interest, 54.4% reported no change, and 21% reported increased sexual interest. Only one-fourth of the respondents indicated that sexual interest was less following SCI; the majority of both men and women desired to develop or maintain sexual relationships.

Though gender seemed to have no bearing on sexual interest, there were notable differences between men and women regarding changes in sexual activity from pre-injury levels. Men were more likely to report reduced sexual activity, 62.3%, compared to only 41.2% of women. It follows that 37.7% of men and 58.3% of the women respondents reported similar or increased sexual contact. Though not statistically significant ($X^2 = 1.75$; $p = .18$), these differences bear notice. Replications with larger sample sizes are essential before drawing conclusions, but it appears women tend to maintain higher levels of sexual activity than men, thus supporting the notion that after SCI, women adjust better sexually than men. Though sensory and mobility losses are equal in men and women, men must cope with erectile, ejaculatory, and of course, fertility problems. By contrast, the ability to engage in coitus is relatively unaffected in women. In addition, females may compensate more successfully for tactile deficits and mobility limitations than men through non-genital contact, closeness, tenderness, and sharing.

The discrepancy between sexual interest and activity for both men and women underscores the need to provide comprehensive sexual education and counseling for people with SCI. As a group, people with paraplegia and quadriplegia continued to be interested in sexual relationships, but activity did not keep pace with interest. Though 75.3% of the people in the sample stated their interest in sex was at least as great as before their injuries, 53.1% reported sexual activity was reduced from pre-injury levels.

Reasons Given for Reduced Sexual Activity

Data were gathered from the 33 mate and 10 female subjects who reported reduced levels of sexual activity. Respondents were asked to respond "yes" or "no" to each of the following possible reasons for reduced activity: (a) frustration or lack of satisfaction, (b) lack of opportunity, (c) physical problems (i.e., difficulties with erections, spasticity, bladder care, mobility, dysreflexia), (d) fear of bowel or bladder accidents, (e) fertility problems, and (f) other (please specify). The resultant data are shown in Table D.1.

Men were more likely to give multiple reasons for reduced sexual activity than were women. The 33 men gave an average of 2.2 reasons compared to 1.2 responses for women. Physical problems affected more subjects (25) than any other response, with 22 (66.7%) males and three (30%) females reporting that physical problems had an impact on their sexual activity. This is not surprising because of the multiplicity of effects SCI has on physical functioning. That a higher percentage of men than women identified physical problems as a reason for decreased sexual activity can be attributed in part to the fact that men are more dependent on physical-genital functioning for intercourse than are women. Men may also be more performance-oriented than women, leading to higher levels of frustration when physical problems are present.

Lack of opportunity was cited as the next most common cause of decreased sexual activity with 17 (53.1%) men and four (40%) women reporting it as a cause. It appeared that opportunities for casual contact were reduced for many respondents and, at the time of interview, they had not adequately developed relationships that would permit higher levels of sexual activity. Others were involved in relationships, but cited sexual conflict with partners as a problem that limited opportunities.

Frustration or lack of satisfaction was reported by 18 (41.9%) of the 43 subjects, with three (30%) females and 15 (45.5%) males citing this factors as a problem. Some people stated they "just do not feel" the same physical urges and desires as previously and had to rely on other mental and emotional stimuli as a result of the diminution of physical urges.

It was surprising that only eight (18.6%) attributed their reduced sexual activity to the fear of "accidents." The fear of a bowel or bladder accident during intimate contact is a major concern for many newly injured people. It is possible, however, that the respondents who availed themselves of the opportunity for extensive sexual education and counseling during their rehabilitation possessed sufficient information to prevent accidents from adversely affecting their sexual relationships.

The six respondents who gave "other" as a response provided explanations unrelated to their injuries. Reasons given included, "I'm just getting older ... My spouse died," and "The kids get in the way."

Fertility problems were cited by five (15.2%) of the men as a reason for reduced activity. Although many men displayed consternation over their fertility problems, the majority apparently did not allow this to prevent sexual expression. Interestingly, at least four of the male respondents had utilized the services of the University of Utah Health Sciences Center Fertility Clinic, primarily for artificial insemination services because they were unable to produce or ejaculate viable sperm sufficiently to impregnate their partners. Because fertility is rarely affected in women with SCI, none of the women in the sample cited fertility as a problem. Finally, it should be noted that while these findings are interesting, the small number of respondents limits the ability to generalize them to others.

Relationship Between Sexual Activity and Emotional Adjustment

The 43 subjects who reported reduced sexual activity were compared to the 38 respondents with the same or increased levels of sexual activity across dimensions of the General Well Being Schedule (GWBS). Respondents' t tests for independent groups were computed to test whether significant differences on emotional adjustment would be found between these groups.

Comparisons of means of four GWBS measures showed statistically significant differences between the groups on the following subscales: feelings of energy (FEELENER) ($p = .001$), cheerful versus depressed mood (CHEERDEP) ($p = .009$), emotional control (EMOTCNTR) ($p = .047$), and overall general

TABLE D.1
REASONS GIVEN WHEN REDUCED SEXUAL ACTIVITY WAS REPORTED

Reason Given	Men	%	Women	%	Total	%
Frustration/Lack of Satisfaction	15	42.4	3	30	18	41.9
Lack of opportunity	17	51.5	4	40	21	48.8
Physical Problems	22	66.7	3	30	25	58.1
Fear of Accidents	7	21.1	1	10	8	18.6
Fertility Problems	5	15.6	0	0	5	11.6
Other	5	15.6	1	1	6	14.0
Total "Yes" Answers	71		12		83	

well-being (OVERGWB) ($p = .005$). In addition, the *t*-value for relaxed versus anxious mood (RELAXANX) neared significance ($p = .056$) as indicated in Table D.2.

In every statistically significant comparison, the group with decreased sexual activity reported lower levels of emotional adjustment. This finding may be explained by the author's experience that most sexually active people with SCI are involved in committed and intimate relationships, whereas casual sexual activity is less common. Interestingly, several respondents who reported the same or increased sexual activity level were involved in tong-term relationships at the time of the study, whereas prior to injury, they had multiple partners.

To assess whether well-being was related to marital status rather than sexual activity, subjects who were married or living with lovers were contrasted with those who were unmarried. No statistically significant differences were found between groups on any of the ISSI or GWBS measures. It would appear then, that level of sexual activity rather than marital status was the relevant determinant of emotional and social well-being.

Those whose sexual activity did not decrease had to surmount significant physical problems, such as bowel and bladder dysfunction, erectile difficulties, and sensory loss before succeeding in reestablishing sexual activity. We speculate that such people are more determined and more emotionally secure, as well as having supportive partners with whom they can achieve a high level of intimacy. Additional research, however, is needed to test the validity of these speculations, especially in light of the small sample size.

Relationship Between Sexual Activities and Social Adjustment

Differences between mean scores of the two groups on the following six ISSI scales were statistically different: availability of frank and confiding relationships (AVFC) ($p = .030$), adequacy of frank and confiding relationships (ADFC) ($p = .019$), availability of social integration (AVSI) ($p = .049$), availability of attachment (AVAT) ($p = .021$), adequacy of attachment (ADAT) ($p = .009$), and

TABLE D.2

MEANS AND T-VALUES ON GENERAL
WELL-BEING SCHEDULE SCALES OF GROUPS

Measures	Frequency of sex	Group mean	*t*-score	*t* probability
FEELENER	Same or more	13.87	3.35	.001
	Less	11.93		
CHEERDEP	Same or more	19.34	2.68	.009
	Less	17.09		
RELAXANX	Same or more	17.37	1.94	.056*
	Less	13.35		
EMOTCNTR	Same or more	13.16	2.02	.047
	Less	12.07		
OVERGWB	Same or more	79.00	2.92	.005
	Less	70.21		

* Not significant

percentage of attachments satisfied with (ADATPC) ($p = .022$), as shown in Table D.3.

These significant differences underscore the relationship between sexual adjustment, and close, intimate relationships and social adjustment. An intimate sexual relationship, with its attendant closeness, tends to foster a climate wherein partners can confide in and be honest with each other. On logical grounds therefore, the relationship between level of sexual activity and satisfaction with social integration makes sense.

The same holds true for attachment. Those with decreased sexual activity had likely lost an important attachment or at least a major component of satisfaction in primary attachments. Some of these people had been divorced since injury, thus experiencing a major loss. Both availability and adequacy of attachment would likely be less in such instances.

PRACTICE IMPLICATIONS

THE FINDINGS OF THIS STUDY support the writings of many authors and document the importance of sexual adjustment following SCI. Of the respondents, three out of four reported their sexual interest was undiminished although the level of sexual activity for many failed to maintain pace with interest. Men seem to be at higher risk than women for sexual problems that diminish the frequency of intimate contact.

The fact that 47% of the subjects maintained previous levels of sexual activity, although many of them had assumed after injury that their sex lives were over, highlights the importance of sex to people with SCI. Many of those with diminished sexual activity commented on the importance of sex in their lives. Two people even requested sexual counseling.

TABLE D.3

COMPARISONS ON INTERVIEW SCHEDULE FOR SOCIAL INTERACTION SUBSCALES BETWEEN GROUPS WITH (1) SAME AND HIGHER AMOUNT AND (2) LOWER LEVELS OF SEXUAL ACTIVITY

Measures	Frequency of sex	Group mean	t-score	t probability
AVFC	Same or more	2.87	2.21	.030
	Less	2.23		
ADFC	Same or more	3.87	2.39	.019
	Less	3.14		
AVSI	Same or more	10.50	2.00	.049
	Less	9.12		
AVAT	Same or more	6.42	2.35	.021
	Less	5.70		
ADAT	Same or more	8.21	2.69	.009
	Less	6.44		
ADATPC	Same or more	73.87	2.33	.022
	Less	61.95		

Respondents with undiminished sexual contact had higher levels of emotional well-being and social adjustment than their counterparts, as indicated by the significant differences between the groups on four GWBS and six ISSI scales. Of particular importance are the significant differences between groups on four of the five major ISSI scales and on the overall well-being scale of GWBS.

Goals in Sexual Adjustment

Before achieving adequate sexual adjustment, many people must reassess their sexuality and expectations for sex. Often, the physical aspects of lovemaking diminish in importance as people concentrate on closeness, sharing, and intimacy. It must be emphasized that the brain, not the genitals, is the primary organ of sexual desire and arousal. Orgasm must not be the goal of sex, but rather the emphasis is placed on the process of lovemaking.

As a result of the erectile difficulties many men experience, coitus may not be possible for many couples. In addition, most men and women with SCI have diminished or absent genital sensation. As a result, genital intercourse may be less important than when genital functioning is intact. Non-genital methods of intimate expression, therefore, take on added importance.

Perhaps the most important aspect of sexual adjustment following SCI is the need for partners to share and communicate openly. Physical capabilities and limitations must be discussed. Obstacles such as bowel and bladder problems must be managed to prevent accidents. Experimentation is critical to enhanced intimacy. It is no wonder that those in this study who maintained sexual activity reported high levels of availability and adequacy of frank and confiding relationships. They had the ability and opportunity to share and problem-solve with their partners about extremely sensitive issues.

The findings of this and other studies indicate that males have more difficulty than females in making changes that enhance their sex lives. In part, this appears to be related to the physical effects that are unique to males. Males may need more help over a longer period of time to adjust to the changes precipitated by their injuries.

Education and Counseling

The findings of this study strongly attest to the need for comprehensive sexual counseling education programs in the initial weeks and months following SCI. At the University of Utah Spinal Cord Injury Center, such a program was developed in 1980 to assist acutely injured people to adjust sexually. Sexual education is provided primarily by means of a five-session sexuality group. Though content is varied to meet the needs of each group, content by session is generally as follows: (a) introduction and overview, (b) sexual and neurological anatomy and physiology, (c) effects of SCI on physical and genital functioning, (d) practical concerns of lovemaking, and (e) emotional and psychological aspects of intimate relationships following SCI. Spouses or other significant others are encouraged to attend, and a supplementary booklet co-written by one of the authors (Mackelprang & McDonald, 1986; Mackelprang & McDonald, 1988) is provided to all participants. The purpose of the group is to provide patients with sufficient information to understand the potential effects of their injuries. Armed with this knowledge, they can then explore their respective sexual potentials and limitations.

In addition to sexuality groups, individual and couples counseling is vital to assist patients in their sexual adjustment. Patients often request counseling for particular problems they encounter after having participated in these groups. This opportunity is of utmost importance, as the problems encountered are extremely variable, even for people with similar types of injuries.

The combination of group education and private counseling and education is often critical to the sexual adjustment of patients. Evidence of the potentially disastrous effects of lack of sexual knowledge on the marriages of those with SCI was provided by David et al. (1977), who found that much of the sexual dissatisfaction experienced by wives of men with SCI was due to lack of knowledge. Educating and counseling patients and their partners, therefore, is essential to prevent unnecessary problems and to counter the tendency for patients to suppress this vital aspect of their lives.

CONCLUSIONS

THE FINDINGS OF THIS STUDY are the first to establish a relationship between sexual activity and emotional well-being and social adjustment. Further research is needed to validate these results, especially in light of the small sample size of the study. A vital implication of these findings is that by assisting patients with SCI to achieve successful sexual adaptions, professional staff of SCI centers also indirectly assist these patients in making more successful overall social and emotional adjustments. It is clear that despite the extensive changes caused by injuries, sexuality remains an integral part of the lives of persons with SCI. Many people with SCI, given time, counseling, and effort, are able to develop or reestablish rewarding and satisfying sexual relationships.

REFERENCES

Bedbrook, G. (1981). *The care and management of spinal cord injuries.* New York: Springer-Verlag.

Berkman, A. H., Weissman, R. S., & Friedlich, M. H. (1978). Sexual adjustment of spinal cord injured veterans living in the community. *Archives of Physical Medicine and Rehabilitation, 59,* 29-33.

Bregman, S. & Hadley, R. G. (1976). Sexual adjustment and feminine attractiveness among spinal cord injured women. *Archives of Physical Medicine and Rehabilitation, 57,* 448-450.

David, A., Gur, S., & Rozin, R. (1977). Survival in marriage in the paraplegic couple: Psychological study. *Paraplegia, 15,* 198-201.

Fazio, F. S. (1977). *A concurrent validational study of the National Center for Health Statistics General Well-Being Schedule.* (DHEW Publication No. HRA 78-1347). Washington, DC: U. S. Government Printing Office.

Fitting, M. D., Salisbury, D., Davies, N. H., & Mayclin, D. K. (1978). Self-concept and sexuality of spinal cord injured women. *Archives of Sexual Behavior, 7,* 143-156.

Griffith, E. R., Tomko, M. A., & Timms, R. J. (1973). Sexual function in spinal cord injured patients: A review. *Archives of Physical Medicine and Rehabilitation, 54,* 539-543.

Guttman, S. K. (1976), *Spinal cord injuries: Comprehensive management and research* (2nd ed.). Boston: Blackwell Scientific Publications.

Henderson, S., Byme, D. G., & Duncan-Jones, P. (1981). *Neurosis and the social environment*. Sydney, Australia: Academic Press.

Henderson, S., Duncan-Jones, P. Byme, D. G., & Scott, R. (1980). Measuring social relationships: The interview schedule for social interaction. *Psychological Medicine, 10,* 723-734.

Hohmann, G. W. (1973). Sex and the spinal cord injured male. *Accent on Living,* Spring, 23-25.

Hohmann, G. W. (1975). Psychological aspects of treatment and rehabilitation of the spinal cord injured person. *Clinical Orthopedics and Related Research, 112,* 81-88.

Mackelprang, R. W. & McDonald, B. M. (1986), *A guide to sexuality for the spinal cord injured person*. Salt Lake City, UT: University of Utah.

Mackelprang, R. W. & McDonald, B. M. (1988). A *guide to sexuality for the spinal cord injured person* (rev. ed.). Salt Lake City, UT: University of Utah.

Masters, W. H., Johnson, V. E., & Kolodny, R. C. (1985). *Human sexuality* (rev. ed.). Boston: Little, Brown.

McGregor, J. A. & Meeuwsen, J. (1985). Autonomic hyperflexia: A mortal danger for spinal cord damaged women. *American Journal of Obstetrics and Gynecology, 151,* 330-333.

Novak, P. P. & Mitchell, M. M. (1988). Professional involvement in sexuality counseling for patients with spinal cord injuries. *American Journal of Occupational Therapy, 44,* 105-112.

Pervin-Dixon, L. (1988). Sexuality and the spinal cord injured. *Journal of Psychosocial Nursing, 26,* 31-34.

Phelps, G., Brown, M., Chen, J., Dunn, M., Lloyd, E., Stephanick, M. L., Davidson, J. M., & Perkash, I. (1983). Sexual experience and plasma testosterone levels in male veterans after spinal cord injury. *Archives of Physical Medicine and Rehabilitation, 64,* 47-52.

Ray, C. & West J. (1984). Social, sexual, and personal implications of paraplegia. *Paraplegia, 7,* 210-216.

Rossier, A. B., Ruffieux, M., & Ziegler, W. H. (1969). Pregnancy and labor in high traumatic spinal cord lesions. *Paraplegia, 7,* 210-216.

Spinal cord injury: The facts and figures. (1986). Birmingham, AL: The University of Alabama at Birmingham.

Szasz, G. (1986). Sexual function in spinal cord injury. In R. F. Black & M. Bausbaum (Eds.), *Management of spinal cord injuries* (pp. 410-447). Baltimore, MD: Williams and Wilkins.

Thornton, C. E. (1981). Sexuality counseling of women with spinal cord injuries. In D. E. Bullard & S.E. Knight (Eds.), *Sexuality and physical disability: Personal perspectives* (pp. 156-165). St. Louis, MO: C. V. Mosby.

Trieschmann, R. B. (1980). Spinal cord injuries: *Psychological, social, and vocational adjustment*. New York: Pergamon.

Woodbury, B. & Redd, C. (1987). Psychosocial issues and approaches in spinal cord injury. In L. E. Buchannan & D. A. Nawaczenski (Eds.), *Spinal cord injury concepts and management approaches* (pp. 175-218). Baltimore, MD: Williams & Wilkins.

Research Study E

THE ELIGIBILITY WORKER ROLE IN PUBLIC WELFARE: WORKER AND CLIENT PERCEPTIONS

Nancy P. Kropf, Elizabeth W. Lindsey, and Susan Carse-McLocklin

The eligibility worker position in public welfare is a stressful one that includes making decisions about eligibility for benefits. As part of a larger state-wide training evaluation, this study examined the eligibility worker position from both clients' and workers' perspectives. Evidence suggests that these workers are able to manage the information tasks of the position without sacrificing attention to the relationship with their clients. It appears that workers in rural and urban settings may face different issues as part of their job position. Implications for education and training of these workers are presented.

IN THE PUBLIC WELFARE SYSTEM, eligibility workers have responsibility to determine AFDC and Food Stamp eligibility. Based upon their decisions, billions of dollars are allocated to millions of individuals and families each year. This position has been identified as one of the most stressful jobs in public welfare because it involves direct contact with vulnerable clients who are often experiencing crises (Siefert & Hoshino, 1985). In current difficult economic times, eligibility workers are dealing with greater numbers of clients who face multiple problems within the context of diminished public resources.

Since the 1970s, the eligibility worker role has changed dramatically with the separation of social services and income maintenance functions in public welfare. With this organizational re-conceptualization, the eligibility worker role began to be viewed by some more as a "technician" role rather than a service provider position (Hagen, 1987a; Wyers, 1983). However, analyses of the eligibility worker position suggest that many workers address other needs of their clients besides solely determining eligibility for service. One estimate suggests that eligibility workers spend about one-half (47%) of their time in direct contact with their clients (Hagen, 1987b).

These demands of and lack of clarity about the eligibility worker position can create stress and conflicts for individuals in these roles. Workers in various public assistance positions have reported burnout and job dissatisfaction (Hagen, 1989; Jayaratne & Chess, 1984) These perceptions can lead to problems in job performance such as feeling professionally unfulfilled, unappreciated, and depersonalizing their clients. Agencies also face the negative consequences of stress and burnout by high error and turnover rates.

Because of these negative factors, many states require eligibility workers to complete training sessions. Petty and Bruning (1980) evaluated training sessions for public welfare workers. Their findings indicate that policy and procedure training improves worker performance by lowering error rates. However, training needs to be more comprehensive than simply educating workers about procedural information. A holistic training curriculum also includes training on interpersonal skills and relationships to clients (Bricker-Jenkins, 1990; Morton & Lindsey, 1986). These additional training components help eligibility workers gain the people-related skills necessary to work effectively with clients (Lindsey, Yarbrough, & Morton, 1987).

As part of a training project for new eligibility workers that included policy and interpersonal skills components, this study examines the relationship between eligibility workers and their clients. The eligibility worker position has been divided into three sets of responsibilities: information processing (collecting data, compiling statistics); the client-worker relationship (interviewing, managing client stress); and working effectively within the agency environment (the culture of the agency and community, relationships with colleagues and supervisors) (Green, 1980). Using this framework, this study was framed around the following research questions: How does using interpersonal skills teamed during training impact the workers' information processing tasks? How do public welfare clients and workers view their professional relationship? Do perceptions of eligibility workers differ by work environment characteristics? The study was specifically interested in rural and urban settings since there is some evidence that public welfare workers in rural communities assume different tasks than their urban counterparts (Ginsberg, 1984; Young & Martin, 1989).

THE NEW ELIGIBILITY WORKER TRAINING PROJECT

THIS ARTICLE IS BASED on an evaluation of an eligibility worker training project in public welfare (Carse-McLocklin, Lindsey, & Anderson, 1991). The training program was instituted in response to the high error rate in both AFDC and Food Stamp programs (Lindsey, In press). All new eligibility workers in Georgia were required to attend a training program which lasted about 20 days for Food Stamp classes and 23 days for AFDC sessions. Training sessions were held in four locations throughout the state. New trainings were started at eight week intervals.

Training consisted of both policy and procedure training and a Casework Skills Training component (CST) which was added in 1989 (Lindsey, 1991). This modification reflected a move from an almost exclusive focus on policy and procedures to an approach which incorporated interviewing, listening, and responding techniques. The CST component of training includes empathic responses, attending behaviors, use of reflective statements, and use of questions. The goal of CST is to instruct eligibility workers in collecting client information in a way that demonstrates warmth, acceptance, and respect to their clients. The training curriculum was a product of a collaboration between the Georgia Division of Family and Children Service (DFCS) and the School of Social Work at the University of Georgia. As a component of the training evaluation, eligibility workers evaluated their training after they returned to work in their own agency sites.

METHODOLOGY

THIS STUDY WAS A PART of a larger evaluation research project concerning the effectiveness of eligibility worker training. The population of this study included both eligibility workers and public welfare clients. The workers were AFDC and Food Stamp caseworkers who attended training sessions held between January and September 1990 and were employed in an eligibility caseworker position at the time of the survey. A random sample of 250 workers was selected.

To provide a true perspective of the worker-client relationship, public welfare clients were asked about their perception of their worker. The client population contained AFDC and Food Stamp clients whose eligibility workers were included in the caseworker sample. Clients' names were obtained from their workers' AFDC and Food Stamp reports. A random sample of 300 clients was drawn.

Data Collection and Analyses

Data were collected through mailed questionnaires. Drafts of both eligibility worker and client instruments were critiqued by an advisory committee comprised of AFDC and Food Stamp trainers, social work faculty, and state and local agency staff. The questionnaires were pretested in February 1991 with twenty-five workers and clients. Eligibility worker questionnaires included items related to the New Worker Training, implementation of the acquired knowledge and skills within their agency setting, and demographic information. Client surveys included demographics and items about their experience with a specific caseworker who was identified on the survey. Both client and caseworker surveys contained Likert-scaled items, rated from strongly disagree (1) to strongly agree (6). Tables E.1-E.3 summarize the individual items from both surveys.

The surveys were designed and distributed according to the Total Design Method (Dillman, 1978). This dissemination strategy includes follow-up mailings and redistribution of the instrument to nonrespondents. The return rate was 90.4% for workers and 68% for clients.

Data analyses were run using the SAS package. The procedures run were frequency distributions and *T*-tests.

RESULTS

FOR THE ELIGIBILITY WORKERS, the average age of the respondent was 30.6 years with a range between 25 and 60 years of age (*SD* = 8.25). Most of these workers were female (84%). Respondents were split almost evenly between eligibility workers who attended AFDC training (*n* = 107) and Food Stamp training (*n* = 99). For the most part, these trainees had been in public welfare for at least one year (55%) and were being trained for new positions. The remaining workers (45%) were employed less than one year. Forty-one percent (41%) of the eligibility workers were from urban areas and the remaining 58% represented rural locations.

Not surprisingly, the client group was predominantly female (90%). Respondents' ages ranged from 17 to 80 years (*SD* = 15.58), with 37 years as the average age of this group. Thirty percent (30%) were from urban areas and the remaining clients (69%) were from mostly rural counties.

Information Processing Skills

Since the New Worker Training sessions included interpersonal skill training, the eligibility workers evaluated how the use of these skills affected their ability

TABLE E.1
PERCEPTIONS OF INFORMATION PROCESSING SKILLS

	M	SD
Eligibility Worker Perception Items[a]		
Inadequate time with clients to implement CSTs	3.5	1.50
Using CST had negative impact on time for other tasks	3.0	1.30
CSTs were irrelevant to job	2.1	.97
Client Perception Items[a]		
Caseworker did everything to determine eligibility	5.2	.91
Caseworker knows job	5.1	.91
Caseworker spent enough time	3.3	1.80
Want to talk about unrelated matters	3.9	1.60

[a]Scale : 1 = strongly disagree, 2 = disagree, 3 = slightly disagree,
4 = slightly agree, 5 = agree, 6 = strongly agree

to complete other job demands. Some workers felt that using their interpersonal skills was time consuming; however, most did not perceive that using these skills detracted from other job demands (see Table E.1 on the following page).

Fewer than half the respondents (47%) reported that there was inadequate time to carry out their casework training with clients. Most of the sample (62%) perceived that using their casework skills did not have a negative effect upon performing other job-related tasks in a timely manner. In spite of the many competing demands of the eligibility worker position, most workers (92%) reported their casework skills were relevant to their job.

Clients also evaluated their eligibility worker's ability to fulfill their job responsibilities. For the most part, clients perceived their eligibility worker as a competent professional (see Table E.1). Clients perceived that their worker did everything necessary to determine eligibility for benefits (96%) and felt strongly that caseworkers knew how to perform their job responsibilities (94%). Clients tended to feel that their worker spent enough time with them (64%), however, many respondents wanted to spend additional time discussing matters unrelated to eligibility benefits with their caseworkers (63%).

Relationships with Clients

Overwhelmingly, the eligibility workers felt that they shared a positive relationship with their clients (99%) (See Table E.2). Responses suggest that the eligibility workers recognized the importance of using good interpersonal skills, as taught in Casework Skills Training (CSTs), as part of the eligibility process in public welfare. This group felt that empathy is important in the worker-client relationship (97%). They also felt that an eligibility worker should convey caring about their clients' feelings and situations (96%). Some (44%) reported feeling frustrated when they were not using casework skills with their clients. When asked to compare their work with clients, a slight majority of trained eligibility workers (55%) perceived that they related differently to clients than untrained colleagues.

The clients corroborated the positive relationship between themselves and their eligibility workers (see Table E.2). Clients report that it is important to have their worker care about them (98%). The workers were perceived as patient

TABLE E.2
PERCEPTIONS OF THE ELIGIBILITY WORKER-CLIENT RELATIONSHIP

	M	SD
Eligibility Worker Perception Items[a]		
Positive relationship with clients	5.2	.65
Empathy is important	4.9	.78
Caseworker should convey caring about clients' feelings and situations	5.1	.81
Frustrated when CSTs are not used with clients	2.8	1.30
Relate to clients differently than untrained colleagues	3.3	1.50
Client Perception Items[a]		
Important that caseworker care about clients	5.3	.93
Caseworker was patient	5.1	.97
Happy with treatment	5.0	1.20
Felt caseworker liked me	4.7	1.20
Felt caseworker listened	5.1	.92
Caseworker understood clients' feelings and situation	4.9	1.20
Felt comfortable with caseworker	5.0	.96
Felt comfortable answering personal questions	5.0	1.00

[a]Scale: 1 = strongly disagree, 2 = disagree, 3 = slightly disagree,
4 = slightly agree, 5 = agree, 6 = strongly agree

(95%), and the clients were happy with the treatment they received (92%). The respondents felt that their workers liked them (86%), listened to them (94%), and that their feelings and situations were understood (89%). They felt comfortable talking with their workers (94%), even when responding to personal questions which are part of the eligibility interview process (91%).

Work Environment

Eligibility workers were asked about how training related to the actual work in their agency setting. Three sets of items were related to this training component (see Table E.3). One addressed the adequacy of the training for their position. A second set dealt with the relevance of skills taught in training sessions to the actual work performed in their job. A third category of items identified barriers in the workplace to using casework skills. Finally, bivariate analyses (T-tests) were run within both the caseworker and client groups to determine if perceptions differed by any characteristics of clients and eligibility workers. These included differences in rural/urban settings, Food Stamps or AFDC programs, and length of time workers had been at their agency.

While the respondents generally perceived that training was adequate, the eligibility workers appear to want more practical training with client related issues. Overall, the group felt that the trainers were effective in teaching content (90%). While most did not want additional training sessions about working with clients (64%), the majority did report that they would like more on-the-job training to work more effectively with clients (56%).

Eligibility workers reported that casework skills are a relevant component of their jobs. These respondents perceived that the skills learned in Casework Skills

TABLE E.3
PERCEPTIONS OF THE WORK ENVIRONMENT

	M	SD
Adequacy of Training:		
Trainers were effective in teaching content	4.8	1.00
Want more training working with clients	2.8	1.40
Want more on-the-job training with clients	3.6	1.50
Relevance of skills:		
CSTs are useful with clients	4.0	1.40
Feel comfortable using CSTs	5.1	1.00
Should receive CST soon after being hired	4.2	1.50
Barriers in Work Place:		
Supervisor values training	4.3	1.10
Untrained colleagues view CSTs as not useful in job	3.6	1.30
Co-workers state CSTs should not be used	2.0	1.20

[a]Scale: 1 = strongly disagree, 2 = disagree, 3 = slightly disagree,
4 = slightly agree, 5 = agree, 6 = strongly agree

Training have been useful (73%) and they feel comfortable in using these techniques with clients (90%). This group tended to agree that new eligibility workers should receive this training soon after they are hired (67%).

The final set of items identified potential barriers in the agency environment which hinders the use of casework skills. Many of the respondents felt that their supervisors valued their use of the skills learned in CST sessions (81%). However, workers generally experienced less support for using casework skills from untrained colleagues. Many reported that coworkers who did not receive training in CSTs thought that these skills are not a useful part of their jobs (57%); however, a few told new workers to disregard these skills in work with clients (13%).

A final analysis was run to determine if either eligibility workers or client perceptions differed by individual characteristics or work environment demographics. The demographic variables were gender and age of the individuals. The work-related variables were the length of time in the agency for caseworkers, the community setting in which the agency was located (urban/rural), and worker position type (AFDC/Food Stamp). Significant differences were found on three eligibility worker items and one client item by characteristic variables.

Differences for both groups existed only by geographic location. Rural workers were more likely than their urban counterparts to find that interpersonal skill training was useful in working with clients [$t = (-2.08)$, $p = .04$]. Rural workers were slightly more frustrated than urban workers when they were not using casework skills [$t = (-1.98)$, $p = .051$]. The rural group was also more likely than the urban group to rate their trainers as effective in teaching the Casework Skills Training (CST) component of training [$t = (-2.55)$, $p = .02$]. One client item reached statistical significance. Clients in urban counties were more likely to state that their workers did not spend enough time with them than clients in rural areas ($t = 2.08$, $p = .04$).

LIMITATIONS

CERTAIN LIMITATIONS OF THIS STUDY have an impact upon the interpretation of these data. One limitation is the lack of a comparison group of eligibility workers to measure the actual impact of training. This situation prevents a determination of whether a difference exists between eligibility workers who have gone through the training and untrained colleagues in regard to job performance and relationships with their clients. However, the majority of trained workers (55%) perceived that they did relate to their clients differently than workers who did not receive training. Additional research is needed to empirically judge if differences exist between untrained and trained workers in their job responsibilities.

Two additional issues relate to the client sample. Although the response rate was high for these clients (68%), it is unknown whether the non-respondents differed from the clients that returned the questionnaire. Secondly, the sample contained only clients who were deemed eligible for public assistance services. These clients have more experience with which to form an impression of their caseworker; however, their view may be more positive than those individuals who did not become clients of the system. Therefore, the interpretations of these data should be limited to individuals who have been approved for service in public welfare.

IMPLICATIONS FOR EDUCATION AND TRAINING

THE FINDINGS OF THIS RESEARCH suggest that interpersonal skills are an important component of eligibility work. Caseworkers view these skills as important to their jobs and clients indicate that the outcome of using these techniques (being respected and feeling comfortable) is an important aspect of the relationship with their workers. Training sessions that omit interpersonal skill building sessions may do so on the false pretense that eligibility workers will not have adequate time to employ good casework skills. About half the caseworkers in this sample indicated that using interpersonal skills with clients diverted time from information processing tasks. The long-term effects of using good communication and listening skills, however, may actually be a time saving strategy for eligibility workers. Clients who feel respected and cared about by their workers may feel more comfortable to provide complete and accurate information during interview sessions. While instruction about policies and procedures is clearly important, this content should not sacrifice the people-oriented skills which are needed in eligibility work.

Public assistance clients tend to view their caseworkers as fulfilling their job requirements. The clients perceive their worker as competent and able to perform the necessary tasks for them to receive benefits. As indicated in other research (Hagen, 1987b; Siefert & Hoshino, 1985), clients may be bringing additional concerns to their caseworker. Most of the clients in this sample wanted to discuss unrelated matters with their caseworkers. Training sessions may need to include content on community resources to enable workers to refer clients to programs outside the agency. Due to the complexity and multiplicity of problems experienced by public assistance clients, training sessions may also need to include information about how to handle serious situations such as family violence.

The training session which the eligibility workers completed was extensive, yet the majority wanted additional training. The sample differentiated training that is more "classroom" in nature from more practical training in working with their caseload. Sessions may need to include more emphasis on applying techniques to actual work with clients. Alternate models of training should also be examined to have workers practice using interpersonal skills with clients. One such training strategy is to include a "mini-internship" in the middle of the sessions so trainees can process their experiences during the second half of training. This model has been used in training nursing home ombudsmen (Schneider & Kropf, 1987).

Perceptions of clients and workers appear to differ slightly by community setting. Rural caseworkers tend to value the use of casework skills more than their urban counterparts. This difference may reflect a difference in the nature of relationships in urban and rural areas. Possibly the smaller public assistance offices in rural counties promote a warmer and more personal environment for clients than larger and more urbanized settings. Urban clients were more likely to perceive that their caseworkers did not spend enough time with them. A number of possible factors could account for this perceptual difference including the nature and complexity of problems that urban clients bring to their workers, the different climates which exist in urban and rural agencies, or the uneven job demands of eligibility workers in rural/urban settings. Training sessions should devote some time to the nature of eligibility work in different agency settings.

While the eligibility worker position in public welfare is a stressful one, findings from this statewide study suggest that these workers are managing well in their jobs. Evidence from workers themselves and their clients indicate that the information tasks of the job are being completed without sacrificing the attention to the professional relationship. Training sessions should stress to new eligibility workers the importance of using good interpersonal skills with their clients. These sessions should carefully help trainees with the task of generalizing "Classroom Teaming" into actual practice with clients and coworkers.

Training curricula need to also pay attention to the context of the agency setting, specifically addressing community level differences between workers. Workers in rural communities may receive training in the more global responsibilities which are often included in their positions. Urban trainees may need training in working with higher caseloads and clients that have multiple problems situations. These distinctions between agency contexts can help workers build the skills necessary for work with their particular clients.

REFERENCES

Bricker-Jenkins, M. (1990). Another approach to practice and training. *Public Welfare, 48,* 11-16.

Carse-McLocklin, S., Lindsey, E.W., & Anderson, R. (1991). *New eligibility worker training evaluation report.* Georgia Department of Human Resources and University of Georgia School of Social Work.

Dillman, D.A. (1978). *Mail and telephone surveys: The total design method.* New York: John Wiley & Sons.

Ginsberg, L.H. (1984). Rural public welfare: Observations from West Virginia. *Human Services in the Rural Environment, 9,* 5-7.

Green, E. (1980). *The hidden agenda: Content and nature of the income maintenance worker's job.* Department of Health, Education, and Welfare.

Hagen, J. L. (1987a). Training income maintenance workers: A look at the empirical evidence. *Journal of Continuing Social Work Education, 5,* 3-9.

Hagen, J.L. (1987b). Income maintenance workers: Technicians or service providers. *Social Service Review, 61,* 261-271.

Hagen, J.L. (1989). Income maintenance workers: Burned-out, dissatisfied, and leaving. *Journal of Social Service Research, 13,* 47-61.

Jayaratne, S. & Chess, W.A. (1984). Job satisfaction, burnout, and turnover: A national study. *Social Work, 29,* 448-453.

Lindsey, E.W. (1991). An integrated approach to teaching policy and interviewing skills to new eligibility staff. (Unpublished document).

Lindsey, E. (in press). An intensive classroom approach to training new eligibility workers. *Journal of Continuing Social Work Education.*

Lindsey, E.W., Yarbrough, D.B., & Morton, T.D. (1987). Evaluating interpersonal skills training for public welfare staff. *Social Service Review, 61,* 623-635.

Morton, T.D., & Lindsey, E.W. (1986). Toward a model for interpersonal helping skills use and training in public welfare practice. *Journal of Continuing Social Work Education, 4,* 18-24.

Petty, M. & Bruning, N.S. (1980). Relationship between employee training and error rates in public welfare programs. *Administration in Social Work, 4,* 33-42.

Schneider, R.L. & Kropf, N.P. (1987). *Virginia Ombudsman program: Professional certification curriculum.* Richmond: Virginia Department for the Aging.

Siefert, K. & Hoshino, G. (1985). Recognizing and helping mentally disturbed clients at intake. *Public Welfare, 43,* 10-17.

Wyers, N.L. (1983). Income maintenance and social work: A broken tie. *Social Work, 28,* 261-268.

Young, C.L. & Martin, L.D. (1989). Social services in rural and urban primary care projects. *Human Services in the Rural Environment, 13,* 30-35.